Tales From A Techie
Funny Real Life Stories from Tech Support

By
Matt Garrett
http://turtletechie.com

Published February, 2014 by Matt Garrett, TurtleTechie.com

Copyright © 2014 by Matt Garrett
All Rights Reserved. This book or any portion thereof may not be reproduced or used in any manner whatsoever without the express written permission of the publisher except for the use of brief quotations in a book review.

http://TurtleTechie.com

For my wife.

Table of Contents

Introduction 7
Section I: Oh, It's On! 14
    Chapter 1: Of course it's plugged in! 14
    Chapter 2: It's off. No, it's on! 25
Section II: Liquid Lunacy 36
    Chapter 3: Crystal Light 36
    Chapter 4: More Coffee Please! 51
Section III: Organization Atrocities 72
    Chapter 5: Spam Queen 72
    Chapter 6: The Over Organizer 88
    Chapter 7: Desktop Disaster 106
Section IV: It's for the Children............126
    Chapter 8: iBath   126
    Chapter 9: The Hammer 142
Section V: Web Browsing Wonders........167
    Chapter 10: I Didn't Click Yes!.............167
    Chapter 11: Toolbar Blues 181
Section VI: Sex, Lies and MPEGS 197
    Warning 197
    Chapter 12: Bathtub Backup...............198
    Chapter 13: Husband's Secret 219
    Chapter 14: Executive V"P" 232
Conclusion 247

Introduction

For many years I spent my days and on many occasions my nights and weekends working away in various Information Technology jobs from PC Specialist to Network Administrator. For close to fifteen years I hung in those trenches setting up computers, networks, writing company systems policies and what have you. One part of every one of those jobs has always been tech support. That's right; in addition to my normal daily duties I was also responsible for making sure all the other employees didn't destroy their computers or the companies precious data.

Now, anyone that has ever been in tech support knows that it is no easy task keeping employees from destroying computers. In reality, it's another full time job. Over the years I have met a wide variety of people, unique in their own ways and all with varying skills when it comes to using and taking care of a computer. There have been the "I need the newest, latest and greatest" people that insist on using the latest hardware and software even though they barely used a tenth of the power of the one generation old system they were using, the tinkerers who think they know what they are doing when they actually don't, people who say they don't know how to work a computer yet somehow can if you get them to think for a half second and all manners of people in between.

Dealing with all these different people with their many different personalities, strengths and weaknesses can be challenging to say the least. You have good days and bad days. There were days that people made me proud and made me think I was actually teaching them a thing or two but there were also those days when I wanted to pull my hair out because of the crazy or stupid things a user did. Come to think of it, I tend to blame all the users for my lack of hair these days. It wasn't male pattern baldness and age that made me lose my hair, it was all the crazy problems and crazy users that made me just pull my hair out. That's my story and I'm sticking to it.

Anyway, over the years I have collected many stories involving all these different users. Mind you, most tech support is pretty routine and nothing really worth remembering happens. But, there are those times when a user does something so stupid, or so crazy, or gets so mad for no reason that the experience just sticks with you. I've retold several of these little stories to my friends and family over the years and more than once someone told me I should write a book.

So, today, I finally follow that advice as I give you Volume I of Tales from a Techy. In the upcoming pages, you will find some of the craziest, funniest and even stupidest stories that I have come across over the years. You will laugh, shake your head and maybe even cry a little. Well, you might shed one tear.

Why am I writing this? If you think I am writing this to make fun of the users and the crazy stuff they have done over the years as way to get back at them for my hair loss you would be wrong. Yes, I want you to enjoy the stories and even laugh at some of the stupid stuff people have done. But, I want you to laugh not to make fun of the people who did it but to learn from their mistakes so perhaps one day when you are in a similar situation you won't make the same mistake that these users did, or maybe you will have a little more patience with your computer guy as he tries to fix your problem. I know,

11

not all computer guys have the best personalities in the world, that's why they went into computers in the first place right? But, most aren't bad guys, just people like you and me. Remember, their job is a tough one but many of them toil at it all day and all night just to make sure things are running smoothly.

    I write this for you all to laugh, learn and appreciate your computer guy a little more. It is my hope that you enjoy these stories and they put a smile on your face with maybe a smidgen of knowledge and appreciation in your head.

    And don't worry, from this moment forward I am changing all the names of the individuals in these stories to protect them. Henceforth, if I am talking about a man his name will be Bill, and if it is a woman her name will be Claire. Oh and if one of you I am talking about happens to read this, thank you for the great stories.

Section I: Oh, It's On!
Chapter 1: Of course it's plugged in!

It was early on a Thursday morning several years back. I remember simply because it was one of those Thursdays when you wake up in the morning and think it is Friday but once you realize what day it really is your entire morning is shot. Needless to say I wasn't in the best of moods that morning so maybe part of this whole exchange was actually my fault.

I had just sat down at my desk that morning and was powering on all of my computers. Yes, I used multiple computers in the office just like I do now. In fact, I can't even remember a time when I only used one anymore. It has been that long. Anyway, it was early and most of the office wasn't even there yet. I am a morning person so I always preferred to arrive at the office early to get things done before the calls came rolling in. Needless to say I was sitting down at my desk powering up my stuff for the coming day and was all set to get caught up on a few things before the day really began when my phone rang.

Now I didn't think anyone had even been in the office long enough to discover a problem. Boy was I wrong. I groaned as I read the clock that said 7:05 a.m. and answered the phone.

"This is Matt," I said as I always did.

"Matt...", I heard with a long silence. I waited a moment and finally said, "Yeeess?"

"This is Claire," she finally said with a twinge of annoyance in her voice as if she expected me to already know why she was calling.

"Hi Claire, how are you?" I asked.

"Not good. I got here early this morning to get some work done and I have been here for over a half hour and my computer monitor does NOT work!"

First, let me say that I was surprised that she had been at the office that long since when I arrived there was only one other car there and I happen to know it was not hers. But, I let her have that one. Although, I have to admit on that particular morning the attitude in her voice quite annoyed me. But I remained calm.

"That's not good," I said.

"No, it is NOT!" she replied with a slightly raised voice.

I had already been disappointed that it was Thursday and not Friday and now I am getting attitude from someone before business is even open so this really bent me out of shape. But still I remained calm.

"Is your computer on?" I asked.

"Of course it is," she replied sharply.

"Ok, is the light on the front of the monitor on?"

"NO!", she quipped.

The next question I asked not so much for the information it would provide me but for the sheer pleasure of annoying Claire with a lot of questions. "So when you push the button on the front of the monitor the light doesn't come on and it just sits there and does nothing?"

She sighed, "Nope, not a damn thing."

Language so early in the day, sheesh. I admit I'm no stranger to the more colorful words in the English language; my grandfather was a sailor so I learned them all when I was still a sweet, innocent, young boy. But at 7:05 a.m.? Really?! Sheesh.

"Is it plugged in?"

That question really got to her. I braced myself as she proceeded to shout at me, "Of course the piece of shit is plugged in it was the first damn thing I checked!"

Now I was annoyed. Here it is not even 10 minutes after 7 in the morning and already a frustrated user is yelling at me. I understand when things don't work it is frustrating. But I didn't break it.

"Ok give me just a minute and I will walk down and see what is going on with it and we will get you a new monitor if necessary," I said.

"Ok," she said. And click. No bye or anything she just hung up in my face.

Well, I took my time. I wasn't on the clock after all. My hours didn't start until 8 a.m. anyway and she had ticked me off. So after waiting about 5 or 10 minutes I headed downstairs to the other side of the building where her office was located. The halls were still dark and I almost fell down the stairs because it was so dark. Looking back I guess I could have turned the lights on but since I didn't want to be walking down there in the first place I didn't bother. Finally, I arrived at her door.

"Morning," I said.

"See, this stupid monitor won't even turn on!"

Not even a hello or hi or hey there buddy. Just down to business. I can deal with that. I looked at her monitor and pushed the button and she was right, the darn thing wouldn't turn on. Then I took a look at her surge protector. Low and behold, the power cable for the monitor was lying on the floor sitting next to the surge protector. That's right. It wasn't plugged in!

So, I was yelled and cursed at first thing in the morning before business had even started for the day over an unplugged monitor. This just irritated me.

"Is it plugged in?" I asked.

"Of course it is!" she snapped.

"Then what is this cable right here on the floor NEXT to the surge protector?" I asked.

She looked down, then looked

at me, then looked down again and paused. After a moment she looked back up at me and the color of her face had changed so much she looked like she had stayed out in the sun too long and gotten a little burned.

"That plug wasn't like that when I called."

"I'm sure it wasn't," I said.

I proceeded to reach down and plug the monitor back into the surge protector. I then stood up and reached out and pressed the power button on the front of the monitor. The light magically turned to green and the monitor came on showing the login screen of your computer. Amazing what power will do for a computer monitor, isn't it.

"You're all fixed," I said as I

turned around and walked out the door. I didn't wait around for a thank you or anything like that. Honestly I didn't expect I would get one anyway and I never heard anything else about it. Until....

About a year later Claire came up to me and said, "Guess what?"

"What," I replied.

"That same problem happened with my monitor only this time I looked down and it was unplugged again. So I just plugged it in and I didn't have to call you."

I guess somehow I managed to make some sort of impression on her and she thought to look before calling. I gave her a smile and said, "That's great, I'm glad I didn't have to walk to the other side of the building just to plug something in." She laughed and went about her normal business of the day.

Remember everyone, whenever something doesn't come on like it is supposed to, check the plugs before you call tech support. I admit we don't mind the easy problems like this but there are times when we are busy fixing really important problems and don't have time to plug things in for you. So always check your plugs before calling and I bet you will be able to fix it yourself.

Chapter 2: It's off. No, it's on!

The weekend had come and gone and it was Monday. Everybody begins to shuffle into work not ready for what awaits them me included. So I decide to head up to the kitchen to grab a soda since I'm not much of a coffee fan and I need the caffeine to get the day going right. On my way up I pass by a row of cubicles. You all know what I'm talking about. Virtually every business has them. Cubicle farms. Rows and rows of nice desks situated inside fake walls that give the illusion of at least a little privacy.

As I am walking by I hear my

name being called from down the hall. I look and it's Claire.

"Good morning, Claire," I called out. "How was your weekend?"

"It was fine," she replied. "Do you mind looking at my computer? It's not working right."

"Sure," I said as I walked over to her cubicle.

"I turned my computer on this morning but there is nothing on my screen," she said as I took the last few steps to her desk.

"Are you sure you turned it on?" I asked as I looked at her computer.

"Of course I'm sure!" she said with a raised voice and a hint of disdain for what she thought was a silly question.

With a slight sigh I looked at her computer again noticing all the lights on the front of the case were off. You see, at the time we used custom built computers that I had put together myself so I knew exactly what light should be on and which should be off without having to double check. It was obvious to me that this computer was simply turned off. The light on her flat panel monitor was on and it was shining orange which should tell most anybody that the monitor is on but it has no signal from the video card. It's a pretty standard signal, after all.

"Well, maybe you hit the power strip on the floor or something because that computer is most definitely off", I said.

"It most certainly is not!", she retorted.

"Yes, Claire, it most certainly is," I replied with a light sigh.

It was too early in the morning for this and definitely not the way I wanted to start my week. I had no idea while driving into work that day that I would spend the very first part of it arguing with someone over whether or not a computer was actually on or off. But, here I was engaging in that very argument.

"Can you lose the attitude and just make my computer work!", she said impatiently.

"Okay", I said reaching down for the power button.

It was at this point that

something happened that I did not expect. As I bent down and stretched out my finger to press the power button, Claire flung her hand in front of mine blocking the power button so I could not press it.

"I told you the computer is on, there is no reason for you to turn it on", she said with an irritated, raised voice.

I paused for a moment and looked at her with a slight grin that I'm sure irritated her even more but I didn't care. Not only was she engaging in a debate over the on/off status of a computer, but also she was now blocking my attempts to prove her wrong and actually fix her situation.

"Do you want me to fix it or

not?", I asked.

"Of course!"

"Then move your hand."

"I will not move my hand. You don't need to press the button to fix it", she said.

Great. Now she is telling me how to fix computers because obviously, she knows better than I do. So I stood up and turned around and began walking away.

"Call me when you are ready to turn your computer on," I said calmly.

"Wait!", she cried. "I need to use my computer this morning."

I stopped and paused for a moment. Sighing I turned around and walked back to her desk.

"Are you ready for me to fix it?",

I asked.

"Yes", she said shortly.

"Okay. May I borrow your seat for a minute so I can sit at the keyboard because I may need it", I told her.

"Sure", she said as she stood up and took a few steps back.

I sat down at her desk slowly and paused for a moment as I looked at the monitor still beaming its orange light from the bezel surrounding its dark screen. I then reached down and pressed the power button on her computer.

The computer sprang to life with the fan on the power supply ramping up and the beeps echoed from the computer speakers as it ran its first checks that all computers run during startup. After a moment the Windows logo appeared on the screen followed by the login window. We had life again. All it took was the push of a little button.

I looked at her and smiled as she gave me an irritated smirk and said, "There we go. All I had to do was turn the computer on."

"I know I turned it on already", Claire said. "You must have done something to make it turn off."

"You wouldn't let me touch it, remember?", I replied.

"Well, thanks", she replied. "I have work to do."

"Okay, Claire. Have a great day", I said with a grin as I walked back to my office.

I must say this. There is indeed a possibility that she really did turn on her computer and then accidentally hit the power strip or maybe even the power cable that made it turn off again or she might have pressed the button quickly but failed to press it all the way so it never came on in the first place. But, we will never know. All I know for sure is that her computer was most definitely off when I got to her desk. Why she insisted on keeping me from turning it on I will never know unless she happened to realize her mistake as I got there.

Unfortunately for her, her attempts to hide her mistake only made her look even more foolish to her cubicle neighbors and me. I have a word of advice for all of you out there. If you make a mistake, own up to them no matter how dumb. If she had just admitted to either being mistaken about turning it on or even accidentally hitting something that would have been the end of it. But, she chose to stick to her guns and claim she was right even after she discovered that she was wrong. Admit to your mistakes and things will always turn out better for you in the end. Sure, it might sting more in the beginning, but owning up to your shortcomings is always best and shows your strength of character. Don't be afraid to laugh at yourself, either. Sometimes we make dumb mistakes that are, for lack of a better term, funny. So, laugh it off with whoever finds out. They will respect you more for it than if you lie to cover it up.

Section II: Liquid Lunacy

Chapter 3: Crystal Light

Every tech guy I know has had at least one user that always referred to their computer as a piece of crap. No matter what computer you gave them, it was a piece of crap. You could spend ten thousand dollars on the latest and greatest computer with multiple monitors, multiprocessors, all the bells and whistles and after one day at this user's desk and it is a piece of crap. Sometimes, however, the computer is a piece of crap not because of something it did, but because of something they did.

It was the middle of the afternoon on a hot summer day and

the air conditioner in the office was blowing full steam just trying to keep up. It did a decent job but it was particular hot out there that day and even the office felt a bit stuffy. Everyone was sitting at their desks sipping on water, soda and everything in between. I had just sat down at my desk with my own drink when the call came in.

"This computer is a piece of crap", said the voice on the other end of the line. No hello, no I have a problem, just this computer is a piece of crap.

I knew exactly who it was and not just because I recognized her voice. It was Claire and Claire always started her phone calls to me with "This computer is a piece of crap."

Her computer was brand new and I knew how much we spent on it. It was definitely not a piece of crap. It was the best money could buy at the time. But, I humored her anyway.

"Hi Claire", I said. "What's it doing now?"

"It just locked up! I can't do anything!"

"Did you reboot?", I asked.

"Of course I did. You taught me to do that before calling", she replied."

"So it rebooted without any trouble?", I asked.

"Yes. But when it came up I still can't do anything", Claire said.

"Strange. I will come see you", I said.

Honestly I didn't believe anything was really wrong but I told my boss I was heading to see PU One. I should explain. This was my first job out of college. I was the PC Support Specialist for the local office of a Fortune 500 company. Basically that meant I was responsible for the computers for about 400 employees. Most of the employees were actually quite savvy and eager to learn more about them so they could perform better. But, there were a few employees that had earned the nickname Problem User otherwise known as PU long before I joined the staff. There were actually three that earned the title. Today was PU One.

I actually didn't mind visiting PU One. Claire was actually pretty nice

39

outside of computer problems and honestly quite beautiful as well. Of all the PU's in the office, she was the one you wanted to visit. In fact, my fellow I.T. guys enjoyed handling her problems for me if I was too busy. But, that day I wasn't so off I went.

As I walked up to her desk she could see me over the short wall by her desk in the cubicle farm and she said, "This computer is a piece of crap."

"I know, I know," I said smiling and looking at what was an unusually clean desk. There were no papers, books or anything really except a keyboard, mouse and a partially drunk bottle of pink colored water.

"So it is just locked up and you can't do anything?", I asked.

"That's right."

"That's strange," I said.

"I know. You just gave me this computer and it is already acting as bad as the other one I had. Can't y'all buy some good equipment?"

"Well, we buy some of the best equipment available", I said. "Let me take a look at it."

"Here look!" she exclaimed as she punched one or two keys on the keyboard and it did nothing.

"I see. Did you try moving the mouse?"

"Of course I did", Claire responded quickly.

I reached over the short wall at her desk and gave the mouse a little nudge. It moved more slowly than I had expected over the desk but the cursor on the screen moved clearly showing that the computer wasn't locked up.

"The computer isn't locked up", I said to her.

"Then why can't I type my username?" she asked smugly.

"Mind if I have a seat?", I asked.

She hopped up quickly and stood behind the chair as I sat down at her desk. The desk was perfectly clean and the wood even seemed brighter somehow. I grabbed the mouse and moved the cursor around. The mouse moved sluggishly over the desk, which I found odd but the cursor was moving around. I let go of the mouse and moved my hands over her keyboard. She had one of the fancy ergonomic keyboards that were all the rage back then. You know the keyboards that are set in an arc and split down the center to better fit to the contour of your hands and wrists? I loved them myself but they definitely weren't for everyone.

    I pressed a couple of keys on the keyboard and nothing happened. The keyboard simply wasn't responding. "Great," I thought to myself. "A brand new keyboard has just gone dead." And then I discovered it. I pressed two more keys down and they didn't go down easy and when it finally did the key stuck in the down position. I turned and looked at Claire.

    "I don't know why it's doing that. I haven't done anything", she said.

43

"Well, this is usually caused by some type of liquid usually coffee with sugar or soda", I replied.

"Nothing has gotten on that keyboard."

"I see."

I then picked up the keyboard from one side holding it at a forty-five degree angle. This caused a pink liquid matching the color of the liquid in her plastic bottle to drip out of the keyboard onto the desk.

"Didn't spill anything in it?" I said.

"Well, um, I didn't spill anything inside the keyboard. Just on it."

It was like she thought there was some sort of invisible shield preventing liquid from entering inside

44

the keyboard if she spilled liquid on it.

"If you spilled your drink on it, the liquid will find its way inside," I told her.

"Well that's just because it's a piece of crap."

"Under that logic all keyboards are pieces of crap", I responded.

"Well it's not like I meant to do it", she said.

"I know. I just don't know why you just didn't come out and tell me. What did you spill in there anyway?"

"It's Crystal Light. I had just made it and didn't have a chance to take one drink of it before I knocked it over and half the bottle went everywhere on my desk", she said. "I thought if I told you I would get in trouble so I cleaned up my desk and wiped the mouse and keyboard down. Then I noticed that the keyboard didn't work. So I had to call you."

"Next time you spill something turn your computer off immediately and call me. Many times we can save your keyboard if we clean it properly right away."

"Okay", she said.

"I will be right back with another keyboard", I told her.

"Will it be just like this one?" she asked.

"No it won't. That was the only one we have like that in the building."

"Then I want this one."

"You can't have that one. It no

46

longer works", I told her.

"That's cause it's a piece of crap!"

"I will be right back", I said while shaking my head.

I walked away a little annoyed and a little sticky from the Crystal Light all over my hands. I grabbed a new plain keyboard that was quite dirty. I referred to it as my punishment keyboard. This is the keyboard that I made everyone who has spilled drinks on their keyboards use. Believe it or not that keyboard has seen quite a bit of use. I also made a stop for some cleaner and towels to wipe up the mess and clean out her mouse that had also been gummed up by the Crystal Light.

"Here is the keyboard you will

be using for a week or two", I told her.

"But I don't like this one", she said rather abruptly.

"Tough. You should be more careful with your drinks."

"But, but…"

"No buts. I will try to revive your old keyboard and clean it properly but I have my doubts since none of the keys are working. If I can't fix it I will order you a new keyboard."

"Okay, but it better not be a piece of crap."

"I'll see what I can do. But, no promises."

Accidents happen. Whether you

are at home or at the office sometimes there is a spill. It happens to everybody at some point. Heck, it has even happened to me. If it does happen to you, remember to immediately turn off your computer. Liquid by itself won't harm a keyboard. It's liquid and electricity that do the real damage. In addition sugars, creams and sweeteners must be cleaned from the keyboard to ensure the keys don't stick on you while you are using them. Your I.T. staff will know the best way to clean and dry out your soaked keyboard that might just save it.

    If you are in an office and this happens don't panic. You won't get in trouble. Turn off your computer quickly and call your I.T. guy and tell him or her the truth about what happened. Life will be much easier for both you and your computer guy if you do. In most cases, a new keyboard will be brought to you while they clean the other keyboard and you might even get your old keyboard back when it has been properly cleaned and dried.

Chapter 4: More Coffee Please!

It was a day like any other. Anyone who has ever worked in an office knows what I mean. People were coming and going. Normal calls were coming in to fix this and that. Just a typical day for an I.T. guy in tech support. But, all that was about to change and before it was over I was going to need a change of clothes.

I was sitting at my desk going through my emails when my phone rang. I picked up the phone and said, "Hello".

"Hey. This is Bill." the voice on the phone responded.

"Hey Bill, how are things today", I responded.

"I'm good."

"That's good to hear", I said expecting to hear a but or something come next. But there wasn't anything. Just silence.

I waited for a moment until it felt awkward so I asked, "Do you need help with something?"

"Yes, I do", he responded. "There is something really strange going on with my laptop."

"What do you mean by strange?" I asked.

"Well, everything was working just fine but now all of a sudden every time I press a button on my keyboard I'm getting strange symbols and Chinese letters on the screen."

"Chinese letters?" I asked a

little puzzled.

"Yes it is so weird. I haven't done anything to the computer and it was fine just a second ago but now everything is complete gibberish. How am I supposed to write anything like this?"

"You are sure you didn't press something or click on anything strange?" I asked. "It sounds like you may have accidentally changed the language on the keyboard."

"No I haven't. Everything was fine while I was typing but all of a sudden it just switched."

"Hrmmm. That's strange. I will head to your office and check it out."

"Thanks."

I proceeded to stop what I was

doing and walked across the building to Bill's office. When I got there I found Bill slumped over his laptop pressing random keys on his laptop. As I walked in the door the room smelled like a fresh brewed pot of coffee. His desk was neat as always and his laptop was in pristine condition. He took great pride in taking care of his laptop, which, of course, made me like him even more because he made my job easier.

"Look at the screen. This is just insane!" he exclaimed.

I stood behind him and watched as he pressed random letters on his keyboard while watching these random symbols and Chinese letters appear on his document.

"Interesting", I said. I believed

it too. I had never seen such a random combination of symbols and letters appear on a screen. Sure, you can change languages and use keys for special symbols. But these were completely random and he wasn't pressing any of the normal button combinations to even create the symbols.

"Let me have a look," I said confidently. "I will try to figure out what has been pressed and we will get you fixed up.

"Thanks. I have a deadline to meet this afternoon so the quicker the better", he replied.

I pressed a few of the keys myself and sure enough the strangest letters and symbols that I have ever seen appeared on the screen. What could this be? I glanced quickly at his keyboard to see if any keys were stuck in the down position but found all the keys in perfect condition. They keys still looked as new and shiny as the day I unboxed that laptop.

"I have to say, Bill, I have never seen anything like this before," I told him. "Just let me check a few of the settings."

I began to run through all of the different keyboard settings and all of them looked completely normal. The keyboard was set to English and no special software was installed that would override the default preferences. I took another look at the keyboard itself and even ran my hands over all the keys trying to find something abnormal. But everything just looked fine.

"Did you try to reboot the computer?" I asked.

"You computer guys always ask that", Bill replied with a chuckle. "No I didn't. Guess I should have before calling."

"That's alright. I will give it a quick reboot", I replied.

So I proceeded to do a full shutdown of the computer and left it off. "I am going to leave it off for just a minute just to be safe", I told him. "While we wait, tell me did you spill anything on the keyboard by any chance?"

"No no, of course not", Bill said.

"Have you accidentally dropped it or anything like that?"

"Definitely not. You can look at it and see the laptop is in perfect condition. It's not even dusty."

"Okay I just wanted to make sure before I look into it even more", I replied.

With a quick press of the power button the computer sprang to life again as you would expect. I watched the boot process carefully to see if I saw anything odd show up but everything seemed normal and in English. The login screen appeared and I attempted to sign on. But, when I typed anything, more of those crazy symbols appeared making it impossible to sign on.

"Great!" I thought to myself. "Now what are we going to do."

I looked over to Bill and said,

"Looks like it is still doing it."

"So, what do we do?" Bill asked.

"Well", I said thoughtfully. "Give me just a minute. I will be right back."

I hurried back to my office to grab a boot disc that would boot the computer up without loading a lot of the software and drivers and bypass the login screen entirely. I would have picked up a keyboard to use as well but we were fresh out of USB keyboards that would connect to his laptop. I quickly grabbed the disc and headed back to Bill's office.

"This disc will allow me to boot your computer up without needing the login and it won't load most of the software so I can troubleshoot the problem a little easier", I told him.

"Whatever you say", he said confusingly.

I opened the disc drive, slid the disc into place and rebooted the computer. It took a few moments but finally I had a nice basic desktop that I could work with much more easily than before. I quickly scanned the different settings and everything looked normal.

"I bet it is some type of virus or malware", I thought to myself. "Bet it works now."

Boy, was I wrong. I created a new document and attempted to type a few words in it. Instead of what I typed those silly little symbols and Chinese characters appeared again.

"What!" I exclaimed.

"What is it?" he asked.

"It's still doing it", I replied. "I thought for sure it would work with the disc."

"I have one more idea before I try borrowing a keyboard from someone who needs it."

"What's your idea?" Bill asked.

"I am going to do a full reset of your computer which includes pulling the battery. We will leave it off for a couple of minutes without power and the battery and see if that clears anything up."

I know it was a desperate move. But, I just couldn't figure out why in the world it was acting this way when there was nothing installed on the computer and it had not been

61

dropped, damaged or had anything spilled onto it. I shut down the laptop and closed the lid. After closing the lid I proceeded to unhook everything he had connected to it and last but certainly not least, I disconnected the power cable.

Now all that was left was removing the battery. I picked up the laptop and began to turn it over. As I turned it I discovered what really happened to his laptop's keyboard. As I turned it I had tilted it toward me. When I did hot coffee that looked as if it was loaded with cream and sugar came rushing out of the laptop onto my shirt and lap. I froze as the hot coffee drained out of the laptop and onto me.

It was at that moment that I

noticed the almost empty cup of coffee sitting next to the laptop. Slowly I turned my head and looked over to Bill who sat there trying to look dumbfounded but only looked extremely guilty.

"So I did spill my coffee onto the keyboard. But look! I cleaned it up all the way. I mean, look how clean it is! I bet it is in better shape than most of the other laptops in the office!"

"Yes", I said slowly. "The outside is very clean. But, did you know that a keyboard is not solid!" I exclaimed. "Why didn't you just tell me that you spilled coffee on it?"

"I didn't want you to get mad."

"So true, because having coffee pour onto my lap after I have worked

63

for over a half hour on your computer wouldn't make me mad?"

"Well, I didn't know it would pour onto you."

"Well, now you know!" I replied quickly.

I admit I was a bit hard on him. Much more so than if he had just told me. But, the coffee was still warm and because of the cream and sugar it was also a bit sticky. So now my clothes were covered in coffee stains and sticky and the laptop still didn't work.

"Sorry. I thought that once I got all the coffee off the laptop that everything would be fine. It did take several minutes before it began doing weird things so I figured it wasn't the coffee but something else", Bill said.

64

"It's okay, I understand."

I couldn't be too mad at him. Well, I could and I was. But overall he was one of the best users I had and was normally very good with his computer. This was just an accident.

"Here's the deal", I began. "There isn't a waterproof seal below the keyboard. In fact, there are many cracks and crevasses for the liquid to make its way into the laptop and that is exactly what has happened to your laptop. Right now all that is damaged seems to be the keyboard but more could fail unless it is completely dried and cleaned."

"Oh, I see", he said. "So how am I supposed to work?"

"I will have to find you another computer to use while we get this one repaired and cleaned."

"How long will that take?" he asked.

"Well, longer now because first I need to try to clean up!" I replied.

I got up and walked out of his office to the closest men's room to clean up. After trying my best to get the coffee out I realized all I had done was make things worse. Basically, it looked as if I had wet myself. A nice look at the office. Sighing I headed out of the restroom and went to grab an old computer for Bill to use.

"What happened to you?" Claire said as she walked by me in the hall.

"Oh, Bill dumped coffee in his computer and it got all over me", I

66

said as I walked by without even stopping.

I carried the old computer back to Bill's office and set it down on his desk. It was an old desktop that we hadn't used in quite awhile but it was all we had at the time so he would just have to make do.

"I can't have a spare laptop to take with me?" he asked.

"No."

"Why not?"

"We don't have any extras, sorry. Besides, you are being punished. So here is your punishment computer and your punishment keyboard. Once your laptop is repaired I will bring it back and we will switch it. This time, keep your coffee away from the computer", I said with a smile.

"Fair enough", he replied.

"I walked out of his office and marched to my boss' office who asked me the same thing as Claire. I told him what happened and let him know I was heading home to change. He said okay with a laugh and I headed home to find something to wear that didn't look like I wet myself and smelled like a coffee shop.

Please, the next time you spill something on your laptop or even the keyboard connected to your computer, just turn it off and call your computer guy. When you do call him be sure you tell the truth. It's much easier for us to fix liquid messes if the computer was turned off immediately and, of course, if we know ahead of time that that is the problem.

Why turn off the computer? It's simple. Liquid won't hurt a computer that is off. Liquid is not the ultimate enemy. Liquid and electrical current are the enemies and the computer equipment is collateral damage. If you have a spill on your computer, turn it off first before you do anything. If you have only spilled water on it, you simply need to dry it out before you use it. If it's something with syrup or sugar, you will need to clean it first and then dry it out before you use it.

This may require you to disassemble the computer first to be sure every single part has been cleaned properly. If you are unsure of how you should proceed, call your friendly I.T. guy for help and he/she will be able to assist you.

Smaller devices can be placed in rice to dry but that isn't practical for a full sized computer. So, you will simply have to dry it the old fashioned way with time. If you can, give it several days to dry out completely before you try to use it. The longer the better really.

Above all, if you do have a spill on your computer especially in the workplace, don't lie to your I.T. guy about it. Trust me, you will get caught. It will be much easier for both you and them if you just fess up to the accident at the beginning. In many cases, your computer can be saved right away and you won't have to wait days and days for a replacement computer or part. While you are working, try to keep your drinks a few feet away from your computer if you can.

Section III: Organization Atrocities

Chapter 5: Spam Queen

If we go back in time several years we will enter a time when Spam was just beginning to truly be a problem. Back then companies, especially small companies, didn't spend hundreds of thousands of dollars trying to combat email spam. It was done the old fashioned way with email client rules and manual deletion. For most people, this was sufficient. With a little education, I was able to inform my users how to minimize their spam risks to keep it to a minimum.

Back then you really would only

start receiving a lot of spam email by signing up for various lists. This happened because companies would then take these lists and sell them to other individuals and/or companies who would then start sending you email that you didn't want about junk you didn't need. Sometimes this was normal, every day stuff and, as you all know, sometimes it was for something a little more adult in nature.

Regardless of what it was you were still receiving email you didn't want. Of course, all these junk emails came with an unsubscribe link that you could use. But, did it really work? Well, what do you think? The reality was and still is that when you unsubscribe to this junk mail all you do is confirm the existence of your email address that will then be sold again and again and again. This, of course, results in a never-ending barrage of unwanted email in your box. Many of these basic practices are still in use today by spammers but back then everything was new and most users out there had no idea how things worked.

I tried my best to educate my users to help them fight email spam. My company wasn't prepared to invest the dollars to fight it yet so I had to make due with a little simple education. Unfortunately, sometimes my education fell on deaf ears.

Looking back people not listening to me did encourage my company to invest in spam scanning.

But, at the time to me and to poor Claire it wasn't very good at all.

I had just arrived at the office from a nice lunch out. For a while I toyed with the idea of eating lunch at the office but after about six months worth of lunches getting interrupted I had given up. The only way to get a break was to actually leave the office. So that's what I started doing. I just sat down at my desk to prepare for the afternoon when my phone began to ring.

"Hello."

"Hi, this is Claire. I saw you walking in from lunch and I wanted to catch you."

I should stop to tell you, Claire

was the executive assistant of Bill, the president and the owner of the company. Needless to say, regardless of the problem, her problems were often his problems so they always made it to the top of the priority list no matter what was going on. The server room could be on fire and I would be fixing a printer for Claire or Bill instead. After that I would put out the fire or call the fire department. That's just how things worked.

"Okay, what's going on?"

"In the last thirty minutes me and Bill have gotten over 500 email messages."

Now, I knew they received a lot of email but even for them that was a bit crazy.

"That sounds like way too much."

"Ya think?" she replied sarcastically.

With a little chuckle I asked, "Are these emails legit emails or just spam?"

"Spam. Definitely. And some of them aren't the most....um....work appropriate spam either."

"Oh, really! Have you or Bill been looking at things online you shouldn't?", I asked jokingly.

"Hahaha no. Well, at least I haven't. I can't speak for him. But I'm looking at my email and his and there are hundreds of some of the nastiest emails I have ever seen."

"Well, let me run up there and

take a look", I told her.

I headed up the stairs and off to the executive offices. I should also let you know that Claire's email had both her email and the president's email. She took care of filtering it out for him so he only had to read the important stuff because he was, after all, a very busy man.

"A little email trouble?", I asked as I walked in the door.

"Yeah, you could say that", she responded.

"Well, let me take a look."

I sat down at her desk and proceeded to browse some of the funniest and grossest spam email I have ever seen. Enhancement pills, horse parts, Nigerian princes,

Nigerian princes with horse parts because of enhancement pills, you name it. There were hundreds. In the last hour while I was gone to lunch Claire and Bill had received over five hundred of these emails.

"Wow! You weren't kidding. That is a lot of email!"

"I know. I just don't understand it", Claire said.

"You two haven't been going around the Internet and signing up for a bunch of stuff you probably shouldn't?"

"No."

"Hrmmm."

"Well, I know he did sign up for a few mailing lists and I have signed up for several shopping sites. But they are all big, well known stores not just some local website I found."

"Oh I see. Well what probably happened is those big sites sold your email addresses and that got you put on some of the lists. But for that this is still a lot of spam. I haven't seen this many before. Look, twenty more just came in while I have been here."

"I know!", she exclaimed. "I've been trying to get off the lists so we would stop getting them, too."

"What do you mean?", I asked.

"Well, when one of these emails comes in, I go to the unsubscribe link at the bottom and fill out the unsubscribe form to get removed.

"You did what?", I asked.

"Unsubscribed. I have been

doing it for days but it's getting so bad all my time is being spend just unsubscribing to the emails."

I let out a big sigh and she looked at me puzzled.

"Is unsubscribing a bad thing?", she asked.

"Do you not remember me telling you about that?", I replied.

"Hmmm. No, not really. I remember you talking about it one day but I don't really remember any of the details."

"Ah I see", I said. "Allow me to explain."

"Okay."

"You should never unsubscribe", I told her.

"Why?"

"When you sign up for mailing lists on sites, even reputable companies' websites, they will often sell your email address to individuals and companies. These companies then send you a little bit of junk email."

"I see", she said nodding.

"Now, when you get the spam, you have been clicking that link and unsubscribing to all this junk email. This lets the spammer know that your email address is indeed a legitimate email address that is actively in use. So, the first spammer who got your email address then sold your address as part of another list to a whole host of spammers who then found and the same thing because you clicked their unsubscribe link. The process repeats itself again and again and again until you are getting over five hundred pieces of junk email an hour."

"Oh my god! I had no idea. I have been doing that on Bill's account as well."

"I know", I replied with a sigh.

"We don't have any spam scanning currently here although we might be able to do something about that now", I said with a grin.

"What do we do right now, though?", Claire asked.

"Well, we are going to have to setup a few rules to filter the mail when it comes in. We will need to set these up on your account and Bill's as well."

"Okay. Just tell me what I need

to do."

"Many of the emails you are getting will only come from an address once as they rarely use the same address. But, if you see an address that comes up several times we can block that. For everything else, we will have to setup some rules based on the content. But we won't be able to get everything."

"Show me how to setup the rules and I can do it."

"Sounds good. I will setup a few for you and then you can work to slowly filter the messages down."

I proceeded to show her how to create rules on her and Bill's account and helped her figure out what to just block and what to scan for so the really nasty junk wouldn't even show up. After about an hour of setup on her account and Bill's account we were finally finished.

"Remember, don't unsubscribe! Ever again!!"

"Oh don't worry", Claire said. "I don't plan on ever unsubscribing to emails again."

"Ok good. Let me know how the rules work. We might have to tweak them a little bit"

"I will. Thank you!" she said.

It wasn't too long after this incident that we were able to install dedicated spam scanning software to help prevent spam. But, in the meantime, the rules worked pretty well but they didn't catch everything. Claire still spent a little time cleaning up until our spam scanning was installed. To this day if you check the spam of Bill's account you will find the horse part emails sitting in his email box waiting to be cleared. I don't know what kind of nasty list that his account got signed up for, but I want no part of it.

Spam scanning isn't a perfect science and it won't catch everything. If you do happen to receive spam in your inbox remember to just delete and move on. Don't spend any time with it at all. It's just not worth it. Whatever you do, do not unsubscribe from one of these unsolicited emails. If it is not a list you specifically signed up for, do not ever click the unsubscribe button. At the very least that button will let the spammers know you exist and things will get worse or, even worse, it could take you to a site that is riddled with spyware and viruses to really turn your day into a big headache.

Chapter 6: The Over Organizer

How many of you remember the good 'ole days of Windows 98? Well I do. Back before the days of Windows XP and Windows 7 there were two choices of operating systems – Windows NT and Windows 98. Windows NT was built with corporate networks in mind and because of this came with all the security you needed to lock down files and folders. But, Windows NT did cost more than its counterpart designed more for home use – Windows 98. Windows 98 could be configured to connect to the same networks as Windows NT so many companies often opted for Windows 98 instead of the more expensive Windows NT. I worked at several different companies and it was the same everywhere at that time.

The problem with choosing Windows 98 over Windows NT is Windows 98 was not designed to be locked down as tight as Windows NT. This left several security issues that could cause problems because users had access to virtually anything on the computer. How bad of a problem could this really cause? Well, you are about to find out.

It was getting to be late in the day and I was hitting that wall that many of us hit. Do you know what I mean? I was tired and couldn't focus very well. Honestly, a nap sounded really nice. Of course, this was work so that was definitely not an option so I ran to the coffee maker to pour an afternoon pick me up. I couldn't have been gone more than five minutes because my office was literally around the corner from the break room – a fact I quite enjoyed. I sat down in my chair and listened to my voicemail.

"Hi, this is Claire. I rebooted my computer and now it won't come on. Can you call me?"

I hung up the phone and paused for a moment. "I think I will just head down there", I thought to myself. So I got up and headed to the other end of the building. Luckily, it was at least on the same floor. When I arrived at the door I opened my mouth to speak but before I got the words out Claire was speaking a mile a minute.

"Oh my god I am so glad you came down here. I don't know what I'm going to do. How am I gonna work? This can't be happening. Why does this always happen to me?!"

"Okay, calm down", I said. "Let me see what's going on."

"Can you see, can you see? A black screen with a bunch of junk on there I don't even understand and then at the bottom it says no operating system found. How can that be it was just working a minute ago."

"Well, it is possible your hard drive went out. I will have to have a look."

"Why would it do that? It was

working perfectly."

"There are a number of things that could have happened. I need to take a look. What were you doing before you rebooted?"

"Just cleaning up my files and directories. Getting everything organized", she responded.

"Okay. Let me give this a quick reboot and see what I get."

"It's just going to show you the same thing. I've rebooted that thing five times now and it's still just showing that missing operating system error."

"I see, I will reboot it anyway and see."

I gave the system one reboot and sure enough it went right back to the no operating system found error. So, I restarted again and entered setup to see if the hard drive was listed. After seeing it in the list and even rescanning for the hard drive everything looked fine. The computer just couldn't find the operating system for some strange reason.

"That's very odd", I said.

"See, I told you. It's crazy", she said. All I was doing was organizing my files. That's it. I didn't do anything. I didn't spill anything. I didn't kick it, knock it over, nothing!"

"Calm down. It's okay we will figure this out."

"Oh I hope the computer isn't dead. I spent so much time today organizing the files. I can't believe how many files were just in random folders. I don't know why I let it get so bad."

"Well, it happens", I replied as I took the case off her computer to check all the cables. "You get busy with work and don't have time to file everything away and then you go back later to do it and realize exactly how many you have and you wonder how you can find anything. I've been there."

"Exactly! I had a little bit of time this afternoon so I thought it would be a good time to get caught up on the filing. I started organizing on the shared drive and got everything just perfect. I'm sure everybody will love how organized the files are now. Not that I can see them anymore."

"Well that's good I'm sure everybody will appreciate how organized the network drive is now."

"Oh I know they will. After I finished the network drive I decided to organize the files on my computer. So I went through my desktop and the My Documents folder and got everything organized there too."

"That's great", I said unhooking the cable connecting her hard drive to her computer's motherboard. "Hrmmm, this cable looks fine."

"Once I got done with my desktop and My Documents I went to the C Drive to sort through files I just stuck there. I cleaned all of those up too."

95

"That's great. If you keep everything organized and off your desktop your computer will run much smoother and you will also find your files much faster."

"That's what I thought, too."

"Of course that will be the case once I figure out why your computer won't boot up", I said.

"I can't wait to use it again. Everything is all organized. It's just perfect. I tell you when I opened the Windows folder on the C Drive and saw what a mess that was I almost freaked. But I took care of it anyway. Now, all those files are in folders according to what they are."

"Wait....You did what?!"

"I organized that messy

Windows folder. I tell you I don't know how it got to be so bad. I feel bad about letting it get that way. Of course, there are some files that I'm not sure about. Maybe you can tell me where I should put them."

My eye began to twitch slightly as I said, "So, you organized all the files in the Windows folder?"

"Yes I did", Claire replied.

"I got rid of a few files that didn't seem to do anything as well. No need to junk up the computer, right."

I was stunned. Still in disbelief I repeated, "So....you...organized the files....in the....Windows folder?"

"Yes, silly. Why are you asking it like that?"

"You do know that you aren't supposed to touch that folder."

"Nobody ever told me that."

She had me. In fairness, she started working there way before me so I didn't forget to tell her. But nobody thought it was important to tell her. I understand why. Most people don't touch folders that they don't know about it. But not Claire. She got on an organizing roll and it didn't matter if it was a folder full of documents or system files she was going to have it neat.

"You should see the folder. Almost everything is in a nice folder. It's so tidy. Why would they leave it such a mess?"

There goes my eye twitch again. "You would have to ask Bill Gates that question. Everything in that folder is there for a reason. That is what makes Windows boot up and run."

"I don't think it was that. It ran fine even after I moved the files", she replied quickly.

"I'm sure it did because everything was loaded into memory so it didn't need access to the files. But, as soon as you rebooted, it went looking for the files and they weren't there."

"Oh. Well, I didn't know that."

"Now you know."

"So, what do we do now?", she asked.

"Did you delete any of the files?"

"I don't know."

"You don't know?"

"I might have", she replied.

"Do you happen to remember the names of the files?", I asked.

"I doubt they were important. Command – something."

"Great."

I was faced with a problem. I could spend the hours it would take to put it back together by hand, or I could spend hours reformatting the computer and setting it up from scratch. The former would allow her to keep everything just as she had it including her settings but there is no guarantee it would ever be the same. Windows 98 was funny like that. The latter would be easier but she would be starting over. I could save her files, of course, but she would lose any custom settings. I chose the latter.

"I am going to have to reformat your computer."

"What? No, you can't do that. I don't want to lose everything I just did!"

"Don't worry, you won't lose your files. I will back all of them up first. You will lose any settings, though such as your wallpaper and any other customizations you did. The computer will be like it was the day you started."

She sighed heavily and said, "Okay I guess if that's what you have to do."

"That's what I have to do."

"Ok. So what do I do in the meantime?", she asked.

"You will have to find something else to do."

With that I proceeded to start the process of setting up her machine from scratch. It was late in the afternoon by this time so I knew this would be a job that would keep me in the office late.

When the clock struck five I heard, "Okay well I'm leaving. Here is my username and password. Thanks for fixing it!"

I grumbled under my breath but said, "You're welcome. I will have it ready for you in the morning. From now on, don't touch the Windows folder!"

"I promise I won't. Even if it is a big mess", she said. "Goodnight!"

With that she walked out the door to head home. Meanwhile, I was stuck at the office for at least two more hours configuring the computer. I reinstalled Windows 98 and all of the applications she used and proceeded to get her account reconnected with the network. I looked outside as the sunlight faded as night rose to take its place. Finally, a little after seven, I was finished. I shut down the computer and turned off the light of her office as I headed back down to my office to see what happened while I was stuck in Claire's office for the afternoon.

My voicemail was full and I had

too many emails to count. Luckily, everyone else had already gone home so there was nothing more I could do for the night. I turned off my computer and packed up. "Tomorrow will be a day of catch up", I thought to myself. With that I headed home.

Keeping your files neat and organized is always a good thing. But, while using your computer you will come across files that should be left alone. If you don't know what they are or if they are located in a folder with the name Windows in it, it's probably a good idea to stay away. Even if you are a neat freak and want everything in its place, those files should remain untouched.

These days it is a lot more

difficult to mess with those files especially in an office environment. I.T. staffs have locked those down so most users do not have access to them. But, there are still some situations that can leave you with access to them at the office and especially at home. If you see these folders, remember that the files are in there for a reason and if you mess with them you could really mess up your computer and even keep it from booting up. If you do accidentally make a change to the files in one of those folders, call your I.T. guy immediately and tell him/her what happened. They might be able to save your computer from failure. Oh and this is the one time that the fix isn't reboot.

Chapter 7: Desktop Disaster

Every computer guy has seen a desktop disaster at one time or another. I bet some computer guys are even guilty of causing their own desktop disasters. What is a desktop disaster? Well, in this case I mean a desktop that is so full of files that you can't find anything. It's true, as we work we are often very busy and just don't take the time to keep our files organized. This can lead to disaster down the road when you are looking for that one important file that you know you sent to your client but they claim they don't have.

Unorganized files can cause even bigger headaches in a company setting. When users simply keep files on their desktop they never make it to the shared file server where other people that need them have access and, of course, in most scenarios users computers are not backed up so your files are at risk if there is a hard drive failure.

It's because of these reasons that most companies require users to save all files on the network drives. Of course, users are people and people don't always follow the rules. Some companies have gone as far as locking down the local computer to prevent this from happening but most still allow saving to the desktop.

Now in all the years I have spent in computer support I have seen quite a few desktop disasters. In fact, long ago I lost track of how many hours I have spent cleaning up messes like these. But there is one that I will never forget.

It was a normal day at the office. The early morning was rush was winding down and the day was settling into a normal, steady pace. I looked at the time on my computer because I was hoping time would pass so I could get to lunch. For some reason I was extra hungry that day. It could be because I decided to sleep that extra fifteen minutes instead of having breakfast. My phone rang and I looked at the caller i.d. to see that it was Bill. Bill was known for his short temper and, well, general unpleasantness. Add to that the fact that Bill wasn't very good at using a computer and you can probably guess that Bill knew my extension by heart. It also meant I regularly had to endure his wonderful disposition. I took a deep breath as I picked up the phone.

"Hello, this is -"

"It's Bill", he said as he interrupted me quickly. "I don't understand why you can't give me a computer that works. I'm so sick of having all these problems."

"Slow down, Bill. What is going on?"

"It's this crappy computer you gave me. I can't find any of my files. I'm so sick of this. Maybe I should call your boss and tell him you refuse to give me a computer that works. He might like to know that you aren't very helpful, either."

I should tell you, he didn't use the word crappy. Now I don't know about you, but I don't respond too well to a threat before I even really hear the problem. Of course, it's not like the threat would have worked. My boss wanted nothing to do with Bill, either. Over the last year or so of working there he had earned himself a bit of a reputation with anyone in the company that worked to keep things going. The office manager, payroll, mailroom, and even us I.T. guys knew how he was and we were all tired of dealing with him.

"Okay back up. What exactly is your computer doing?", I asked with as much patience as I could muster.

"It's just sitting here. It hasn't crashed or anything like that although I'm surprised it hasn't. It's piece of junk."

"So what are you trying to do?"

"I already told you. I'm trying to find my files but I can't find anything."

"Where did you save them?"

"On the computer!", he responded with a raised voice.

"Very helpful", I thought to myself.

"Okay let me come down there and have a look", I told him.

No sooner had I gotten the work "look" out of my mouth when I heard the phone click. Pleasant to the very end, this one.

"That was Bill!", I called out so my boss could hear. "Guess what? He has a problem!"

"Good luck with that one!", my boss called out with a chuckle in his voice.

"Just so you know he might call you because I gave him a piece of junk computer and I don't help."

"Okay I set my phone to go to voicemail. Good luck fixing his problem this time. What is it anyway?"

"I don't really know. He said he couldn't find his files or something like that."

"Have fun playing hide and go seek!"

"Thanks", I said laughing.

I grinned as I walked out of my office feeling a little better that my boss knew what a pain Bill could be. I took my time. I know I shouldn't admit that to you but he irritated me so I wasn't going to rush. As I walked down the stairs I ran into a couple of people from accounting.

"Where are you off to?", they asked.

"Bill has a problem."

"Oh! Good luck with that one", they said with a grin.

"He's my top priority."

I continued to make my way down the stairs as I listened to the laughing. Accounting knew how he was too, after all. Finally, I reached my destination. I slowed my pace a bit and took a deep breath wanting to maintain my cool as I dealt with him.

"Hey Bill", I said as I walked up to his door.

"Come over here and look at this damn thing."

"Okay."

"I can't find any of my files!", he exclaimed.

"Well, let me see if I can find them", I said as I moved around his desk so his desktop was in full view.

It was then that I saw it. His desktop was a sea of icons. Every inch of his nineteen-inch monitor was covered with little icons. There were files of all types there – image files, documents, spreadsheets, presentations, zip files. Every possible file type you could imagine. It was a jumbled mess of icons.

"Wow!", I exclaimed almost involuntary.

"What?", Bill asked.

"That's a lot of files on your desktop."

"I know. But I can't find the file I'm looking for right now!"

"Did you do a search?"

"Of course I did. I'm not an idiot. You were the one who taught me how to search for files in the first place. Don't you remember?"

"Well, are you sure you are remembering the correct filename?"

"No. But that's not the point. The point is I can't find the file I need!"

"Okay well let's move these files around and see if we can track it down."

It was then that I truly discovered what I mess his desktop really was. I moved one of the icons over to the right only to discover another icon for a file below it. I then moved that file over only discover yet another below it. And then another, and another, and another. I don't know how long it took me to before I saw blank desktop but I know I moved at least twenty files over. I was astonished. Had he not been storing anything on the server even after he was told exactly where to save files?

"There are so many files. How do you find anything?"

"Normally I can find everything without and problem. Just not today."

"You do know that these files are all client related and are supposed to be stored on the file server and not on your desktop."

"I don't like storing things on the server."

"It doesn't matter what you like, that is company policy."

"I will store files where I want to store them!"

"As I told you in your orientation, all files that are company and/or client related are to be stored on the file server so we can ensure the safety and integrity of the data."

"I like saving my files on my

desktop so I have quick access to them."

"But what if someone else in your department needs access to them and you aren't here?"

"Well, that won't happen. Only I need these files. Other people shouldn't be accessing them at all."

"But these are files that are for our clients someone else might need these."

"Then they can make their own. And you can't tell me where I can save files. This is my computer and I will put things where I want them."

I knew I wasn't going to be able to get through to him and now he had made me angry. I always try to be open minded and patient with users and I pride myself on not only helping users fix their problems but also teaching them about the problem they encountered so they learn from the situation regardless of whether or not it was their fault or not. But there was no getting through to Bill. He was stubborn, arrogant and in many ways just a bully. Today, though, I had the bully right where I wanted him.

"You are in violation of our company's digital asset policy. You have a choice. You can either clean up and organize these files on the file server where they are supposed to be stored, or I will report you for violation of the policy", I said with a small grin I just couldn't hide.

"You aren't going to do anything

like that. Now just find my file for me."

"No."

"What did you say to me?", he asked almost surprised.

"I will not help you find the file."

"Yes you will or I will call your boss", he said as he picked up the phone.

"Go ahead. But remember this. When he talks to me about this incident he will find out about your violation and it will then get escalated to the next level."

"Fine. Just help me find my file", Bill said.

"No. This is your mess. You are going to have to clean it up. I expect you to go through all this mess of files and put them into their proper place on the file server."

"Are you kidding me?"

"No I'm not", I said. "I expect all of these files to be cleaned up and put on the server. I will be checking back to make sure you did it, too. Do not just dump them onto the server in a folder with your name on it either. They must be filed according to your departments standards so they can be found and used by other people should the need arise."

"That will take forever."

"You should have thought about that before you made this mess. Oh, I am willing to bet that you will find the file you are looking for while you are cleaning up that mess."

"Fine."

With that I walked out of his office feeling very satisfied. By the time I got back to my office I could hear my boss on the phone. I already knew who it was.

"He's right, Bill. He's not responsible for your mess. Now clean up your files. If, after cleaning up, you still can't find your file, we will come do a search. But, considering you didn't store the files in the proper way in the first place, we might have a hard time finding anything. That is one reason why we require you to store the files in the proper way."

I laughed to myself and headed into my office to catch up on what I missed while I was gone. The next day I returned to Bill's office to check on his progress.

"I put all those files onto the server. Have a look."

I moved around his desk to see a nice clean and very empty desktop. I reached down and opened the server and he showed me some of the files he had moved.

"That's good. When did you finish it?"

"I moved most of them yesterday and finished them up this morning. I hate this. It takes forever to open anything", Bill complained.

"It's just one or two extra clicks. You will get used to it", I said. "Did you find the file you needed?"

He rolled his eyes. "Yes", he begrudgingly said.

"I knew that you would. Thank you for putting all those files in their proper place."

"You're welcome."

There are two lessons that can be learned from this story. First, always keep your files organized. I realize that it is hard when the day is moving fast and you are so busy you don't even have time to blink let alone save files in their proper place. But, it is important to take a little time out of the day to move the files where they need to be so that you can do your part in keeping your company's data safe.

Second, never threaten an I.T. guy - especially one that is really trying to help you. It's a good way to ensure that you won't get the help that you need. Remember, it is not your I.T. guy's fault when something goes wrong. He/she will help you fix the problem so you can get back to work. The two of you are in this together and working for the same goal. So be nice about it. Your I.T. guy will appreciate it and chances are you will get the help you need even faster the next time.

Section IV: It's for the Children

Chapter 8: iBath

Every I.T. guy knows that his/her work is never truly done. Anyone who has ever worked in I.T. support is used to it. As soon as anybody finds out you work on computers you can expect a question. Friends and family members come to you for help at all hours regardless of what is going on in your life. It is just a way of life. In fact, some of the craziest questions and funniest stories have come not from the office, but from my friends and family members.

The release of the iPad caused a

dramatic shift in the way people use computers. In the months after its release computer manufacturers everywhere were releasing their own lines of tablets, which began the era of mobile computing. Today, people everywhere take their computers with them wherever they go. This new era has not only changed the way we adults use computers, but it has changed the way our children use them as well. These days, kids everywhere are swiping their tiny fingers across screens to learn math, read books, watch movies and videos, and, of course, play games.

As time has passed the age of children with access to these devices has gone down and kids under three years old and younger are able to easily use these touch screen devices. More and more apps have been released tailored specifically for very young children as well and a whole new world has been opened to them that previous generations simply did not have access to. In my opinion this is most definitely a good thing. But sometimes, it can be bad. You see children that young don't understand that these very expensive devices cannot be treated like that cheap plastic toy. I have seen iPads tossed, stepped on and even slammed to the floor. Sometimes they survive. But sometimes they do not.

It was about eight o'clock in the evening and my family and I were cleaning up from dinner. Dinner was a bit later than normal on this particular evening because we spent the earlier part of the evening shuffling kids back and forth to after school activities such as soccer practice and dance. My phone rang as I was putting away the dishes. I quick glance on the caller i.d. showed that it was my cousin, Claire.

    Claire has a child, Bill, that isn't quite three yet. And like most children his age, he is quite adept at using an iPad. He watches videos and plays games like many kids his age and absolutely adores his iPad. He also likes to throw his iPad. I have winced more than once as I watched his iPad go crashing to the floor because he decided that is where it needed to be. Originally, Claire only had a basic leather case on the iPad. Each time he threw his iPad I just knew that the screen was going to crack. But, it didn't. Even though it hadn't cracked.... yet.... I still recommended she invest in a case that was designed to protect the device from drops. She, of course, followed my advice and got one of the best cases you could get for the iPad. I remember when she called and told me about it. I slept much better that night knowing I wasn't going to get a call about a broken iPad. Little did I know that I was wrong.

The phone rang a couple of times while I dried my hands before answering.

"Hello", I said.

"Hey, this is Claire."

"Hey there. How are you?"

"Um, I'm okay."

"How's Bill?"

"Oh he's not too happy right now", she replied.

"Really? Why?", I asked.

"I don't know what to do. We were getting ready for his bath and he was watching his iPad. Then for no reason at all he decided to throw it right into the bathtub."

"He did what?"

"Yep, right into the bathtub full of water."

"Wow."

"But I scooped it out of the water really fast. It might have been in there for about two seconds", she said.

"Okay did you turn it off?", I asked.

"Well, it went off on its own."

"Uh-oh. Okay do you have any rice in your cabinets?", I asked quickly.

"Yeah, I think so."

"Okay quickly go find the rice and pour it into a large bowl. Take the case off the iPad and bury it in the rice."

"Why?"

"The rice will pull the moisture out of the iPad."

"Really? I didn't know that. Can I turn it on just to check it first?", she asked.

"No, no no. Just leave it off."

"Okay. Why can't I turn it on?"

"Electricity and water don't mix", I said quickly.

"Good point. Hold on one sec."

I waited for about five minutes and I began to wonder exactly what was going on. It shouldn't take that long to bury an iPad in rice. Finally I heard her pick up the phone.

"I can't get the case off."

"You can't?"

"No it's stuck. How do I get this thing off?"

"It's snapped together. Start at one of the corners", I told her.

"I just can't get it."

"Hang on one sec", I said

frantically as I pulled up Google. Quickly I tracked down a video showing exactly how to put her case on and take it off again. "I'm sending you a video. It shows you exactly what to do. Skip ahead to the second half of the video to see how to take it off."

"Sounds good. Hang on."

I sent her a quick text with the video link so she could watch and I could hear her watching the video.

"Wow this case is hard to get off."

"Yeah but that's one of the reasons it protects the iPad so well. Of course, it's not built to be waterproof. That's why you have to get it off and get the iPad into the rice."

"Ok I got it", she said after about five minutes of fiddling with it.

"Great. Now toss the iPad into the rice and cover it up completely."

"Done", she said after a minute.

"You can go ahead and dry out the case now and just set it aside for now."

"Just let me grab a towel...Okay done. Now I can take the iPad out of the rice?"

"No. It needs to stay in the rice for at least twenty four hours", I said.

"An entire day?"

"Yes."

"But what will Bill do in the meantime?", she asked.

"He will just have to wait. The

longer in the rice the better if you want to be sure it is completely dry."

"Great. He is not going to be happy", she replied.

"Let's just hope that the water didn't destroy the iPad. You could be looking at a dead iPad. We won't know for sure until you give it plenty of time to dry."

"So wait an entire day?"

"Two would be even better. But one day, minimum."

"Great. Well I will try it tomorrow night and let you know."

"I hope it's not dead. If it is, you will have to replace it, most likely."

"Well, let's hope it's not dead then."

"Oh I hope not."

"Okay well thanks. I will call you tomorrow and let you know what happens", she said.

"Sounds good. Talk to you tomorrow."

"Bye", she said.

"Bye."

One day passed and we were again into another evening when my phone rang. As I expected it was Claire.

"Hello."

"Hey it's me", she said.

"Hi. So have you tried it yet?", I asked.

"I just did, actually."

"And…"

"It works!" she said excitedly.

"That's great!"

"Bill is happy he has it back. He's watching his favorite show on it now."

"Well, I'm glad the water didn't destroy it."

"Me too", she responded.

"So, have we learned something from this experience?"

"Yep. Do not bring the iPad around at bath time!"

"Exactly. The just aren't built for water", I said with a chuckle.

"No kidding", she said laughing.

"Well I'm gonna get going. I just wanted to let you know that everything is working. Oh and thank you for the tip."

"No problem at all. Tell Bill I said hi."

"I will", she said. "Talk to you later."

"See ya later."

With that she hung up the phone. I'm not sure if she has really stuck to the no iPad around the bath rule. But at least this one time I know the rice trick actually worked. She saved it too with her quick thinking to get it out of the water as fast as possible.

Remember everyone; iPads and other tablets are great tools for both learning and entertainment for adults and children alike. But, unlike adults, children do not understand that the devices can't simply be tossed around like a toy. A plastic toy suffers no damage from getting wet in a bath full of water, but an electronic device is not so lucky. Water can do a lot of damage to these devices and unless you have extended warranty protection on the devices most places will not replace them if they have been exposed to water. Most of the devices actually have strips that change color inside them if they have been exposed to water so when you take it in for repair they will know.

If you have young children, I encourage you all to do your best to keep these devices separate from bath time. Invest in a good case and maybe even one that is at least somewhat water resistant so you can properly protect your device from water damage and, of course, other types of damage that can be inflicted on these devices in the hands of young children.

By all means give your children access to these devices if you can. They are great tools for learning to read, write and even learning basic math skills. In addition, they provide a great source of entertainment for you child through videos and games. But, if you are going to let your children access these devices, be sure you take as many steps as you can to prevent disasters like this one from happening.

Of course if disaster does strike, remember to keep a box of rice in your cupboard just for this occasion.

Chapter 9: The Hammer

Children often say and do the darnedest things especially when computers are involved. Who really knows what is going through their minds when they decide to do what they do. It is now time to explore the mind of one particular child that I nicknamed, The Hammer.

For many years I worked for a privately owned company. The company had been around for many years and was currently owned by the original founders grandson, Bill. Bill was focused, highly talented and, like so many company owners, worked all the time. Despite working as much as he did he did take pride in spending as much time as he possibly could with his kids. Of course, he couldn't be with them all time and sometimes things went wrong that were totally out of his control.

    One of the many differences you will find when you work in a privately owned company especially if you are in computer support is you will not only be repairing company owned equipment, but the owners personal computers, printers and more. Over the years, I found myself spending a great deal of company time at Bill's house setting up wireless networks, connecting printers and even programming remotes and meeting cable and satellite installers. Personally I didn't mind. It was time out of the office that I was still payed for and at the end of the day, whether it was equipment in the office space or at his house, it was all his stuff and I was paid to keep his stuff working.

    One morning I was sitting at my desk enjoying a soda while I went through the day's emails and tasks when my phone rang. I glanced at the caller I.D. and it was Bill. Of course, he was the president and the owner of the company so I answered it right away. Sorry everybody, but the owners always get the best of treatment. After all, they sign the paychecks.

    "Hello", I said.

    "I've got a bit of a problem", Bill said plainly.

    Bill was, as I said, a very busy

man so he never took the time for any of the normal pleasantries that you might expect on the phone. I didn't mind. After you spend as many hours as I had at his house I knew him pretty well. I lost track of how much of his beer I had drank over the years while working late at his house.

"It seems my son has done something to my laptop at home. My wife just called in a panic about the laptop and said it isn't working", Bill said quickly.

"Okay. Do you know what its doing?"

"That's all I know. Will you run over to the house and see what's going on with it and fix it?"

"Sure. Let her know I will be there in just a few minutes."

"Thanks."

And that was the extent of the conversation. I had no idea what I was walking into. I quickly gathered up a few tools and a bit of software that I thought I might need to repair whatever happened and headed out for my little mid-morning road trip.

Bill lived about ten minutes from the office but with traffic it took me a little longer than I thought to get there. I pulled in and gathered up my I.T. emergency kit that I had brought and began my walk to the door. Before I could even reach the door it was opened for me and his family was standing at the door waiting to greet me.

"Thank you so much for coming over", his wife said.

"Oh no problem at all."

"My computer won't turn on. If I have lost my files I am going to be sick", she said.

"Well, let me take a look."

What I saw next I wasn't prepared for at all. Now, I thought I had seen everything when it came to damaged computers. But, I must admit, this was most definitely a first for me.

The laptop sat closed and I could see a few pieces of plastic around it on the desk. There was a circular mark on the top of the laptop with a huge chunk of plastic missing. I opened the laptop to find two more marks just like the one on the top with the added bonus of a nice crack in the plastic case. I touched one of the marks and tiny, rough pieces of plastic moved out of the mark as I rubbed my finger over it.

"What in the world would do this", I thought to myself.

I pressed the power button on the computer and heard it come on but nothing was coming on the screen. I definitely hadn't brought enough stuff with me to fix this here.

"Do you know what happened?" I asked.

"Well, it seems my little guy here thought it would be fun to hammer the laptop."

"Wait. He what?" I asked.

She read the look of shock on my face and shook her head. "Yeah he decided to hammer the laptop."

"Ha- hammer it?" I stuttered.

"Bet you have never seen this one before", she said with a nervous chuckle.

"I can't say that I have."

"If I lose my files I am in big trouble. I need everything on there."

"Well, I know it is coming on at least because the light is on. But I have no idea if it is booting up and it is just the screen that is broken or if there is something else wrong."

"What about my files? I have pictures of the kids and work files. My whole life is on that laptop."

"I will have to look at the hard drive to know for sure. Give me just a minute let me take the bottom of the case off and have a look inside."

"Alright. Would you like something to drink?"

"No thanks, I'm fine. Let's have a look here, shall we?"

"Sounds good. I hope you can save all my stuff."

Honestly I had no idea if I could fix it or not and one of the hammer marks was right above where the hard drive on the laptop was located with the other mark right above the DVD burner. Chances are something didn't survive. I pressed the power button to turn off the computer and unplugged it. Slowly I lifted it up and turn it over. As I turned it over, I heard something fall inside the laptop. It sounded like plastic or metal moving down from one side of the case to the other as I flipped it over.

"Oh, this can't be good", I thought to myself. I sat it gently on the desk and took the battery out and proceeded to remove all the screws to remove the back case. One by one I removed the tiny screws until I could lift off the back of the case. What I found wasn't good.

There was a chunk of plastic that connected the motherboard to the case that was completely dislodged and there was a crack in the motherboard. I glanced over at the DVD drive and it there was a long crack straight down the middle of the drive. "That drive is toast", I thought. The hard drive looked relatively unscathed by The Hammer. It was then that I heard a small voice.

"I fixed it!" he shouted.

"That's right. You fixed it, alright", I said laughing to myself.

I took one look at the small child who was proud of his accomplishment. His eyes told me everything. You could see the mischievous thoughts running through his mind right in his eyes. He knew exactly what he was doing and from the looks of things enjoyed hammering the laptop.

"I can hammer it some more. I will help!" he exclaimed.

"No, no. That's okay. I will take it from here. Thanks for getting things started", I replied hoping he wouldn't slam the hammer onto the completely exposed hard drive.

"That's enough go play with your toys. I will be up in a minute", his mom said and with that off he went.

I sighed in relief as the small boy ran happily to his room to play with his toys or plot a take over of the world. Whichever it was.

"The good news is the hard drive looks to be in good shape. But I won't know for sure until I remove it and try to connect it to a different computer."

"What does that mean?" she asked.

"That means I'm betting that your files are safe and I can recover them."

"Oh thank god."

"But, the computer. Well...that is a different story", I said honestly.

"How so?"

"I know for sure the DVD drive is dead. It's cracked almost in half."

"Great."

"Also there are some chips on the motherboard which may or may not be bad. It's hard for me to tell for sure here. There is a good chance the screen is also broken beyond repair and will have to be replaced."

"Will that be expensive?"

"Well, this is a Mac so the parts won't be cheap at all. It will be several hundred dollars to fix everything but it can be fixed."

"I don't want to fix it. Let me call Bill."

"Okay."

She picked up the phone and dialed Bill at the office. He was in a meeting as he often was but she is the president's wife so he had him leave the meeting so she could tell him my diagnosis.

"Hey Bill. Matt says the computer is going to cost several hundred dollars to fix. We need to get a new one. But I need one today."

She listened on the phone for a minute then looked at me. "Bill wants to talk to you." Before she handed the phone to me she said, "I want a good one."

"Hello."

"Okay how much is it really going to cost?"

"It's hard to say for sure unless I take it to a Mac shop to find out the cost of the parts. But it won't be cheap."

"Does it really make sense to get a new one?" he asked. He was always very practical with money even though he didn't suffer from a shortage of funds by any means.

"Well, by the time you spend the money to fix this one you could have spent a little more for a new one. It's hard to say exactly how much more. But, with this much damage I wouldn't trust this one again if it were me", I told him honestly.

"That's good enough for me. Go grab one. But, don't get the best one out there. Find one that's used if you can."

"I can definitely do that."

"Just let me know how much it was. Oh, are you going to be able to save the pictures and videos?"

"I think so. I won't know for sure until I get the hard drive back to the office but it looks like it is in good shape."

"Good. So, what happened exactly?

"Well it seems your son decided the laptop needed a little bit of work this morning and took a hammer to it. At least three good strikes that I can see for certain."

"A hammer?" he gasped.

"Yep, a hammer."

"Damn."

"I know. This is a first for me."

"Hey, it's me you're dealing with. You knew it would be something crazy," he joked.

"You got that right. I will grab what's left of this laptop and run out to pick up another one. Then I will have to bring it back to the office to rescue the data."

"Whatever you have to do. Can you get it done today?"

"Maybe. It will depend on how quickly I can find another laptop", I said. "But I will try."

"Great. Just let me know."

"I will swing by your office later."

"Great. See ya. Oh, don't tell her I said get a used one."

"You got it."

With that he hung up and hurried back to his meeting leaving me to clean up the parts of the laptop.

"I will take this one with me to pull the data and I will head out to pick up a new laptop for you. Don't worry, I will get you a good one."

"Thanks", Bill's wife said.

"I might have it ready today. But it might be tomorrow. It's hard to say just yet."

"As long as you can save my files today or tomorrow will be fine."

"I will send it home with Bill when its ready and if you have any questions you can just call me and ask once you get it."

"I will."

"Let's just keep The Hammer away from the new one."

"I know right!" she replied.

I headed out with the broken laptop for my extended road trip. I had to find a laptop that was most definitely better than her old one but wasn't brand new either because Bill didn't want me to spend anymore than he had to spend. My search led me into two stores but in the second I quickly found a used Mac that was like her old one but newer and wasn't going to cost an arm and a leg. I bought it and headed back to the office.

Sitting at my desk with the broken laptop I started to take it apart. Plastic fell from everywhere. There was little doubt in my mind that this computer would have been quite expensive to repair. Amazingly, the hard drive was in perfect condition. I fitted it into a nice external case and connected it to the new laptop. In just a few seconds the hard drive icon appeared on the screen and I was able to copy all the files from it to the new computer. "Bill will be happy about this", I thought. The end of the day was approaching so I grabbed the new laptop and headed for Bill's office. Claire was there as always.

"Hey Matt."

"Hi Claire."

"Is that his wife's new laptop?"

"Yep it is. Let's hope The Hammer doesn't try to fix this one."

She laughed. "I love that nickname for him. It's perfect! You can head on in."

"Matt!"

"Hey Bill."

"Did you get me fixed up?"

"I did. Everything is on this new computer."

"Thank god. Great. What was the damage?"

"Not as bad as I thought it might be", I said as I handed him the receipt.

"Well, no choice I guess", he said shaking his head.

"Not really. Just keep The Hammer away from this one", I said with a chuckle.

"The Hammer?"

"Yeah. That's what I've been calling your son all day."

"That's just perfect", he said with a laugh."

"You know that's what I will call him from now on?"

"Oh I know", he replied. "I might call him that too. Of course, this isn't the worst thing he has done."

"It's not? He's only four."

"I know. A few months ago he stopped up the drains in the bathtub and the sink in the upstairs bathroom. He turned the water on and shut the door."

"Wow. Was there damage?"

"You could say that", Bill said.

"What happened?" I asked.

"Well my wife didn't know he did it because she was downstairs all morning. Then the ceiling caved in below the bathroom."

"Holy!" I exclaimed.

"That's what I said only with a few other words after that."

"That's just crazy. So I guess this computer was just a small thing in comparison to that."

"Yeah."

"Well, I guess you got to watch The Hammer around computers and bathrooms, huh."

"You got that right", he said with a laugh. "Thanks for getting this fixed for me. I appreciate it."

"Oh no problem. Just have your

wife call me if she has any questions."

"I will. Thanks."

Children and computers can be a dangerous mix. Computers can be a great tool of both learning and play for kids of all ages. But sometimes, they can do a great deal of damage to them if you aren't careful or you have one with a little streak of mischief in them like The Hammer. It's important that you teach them early that you can't treat a computer like a plastic toy. Like anything, children need to be taught how to properly use and care for a computer as early as you can. That way you don't run into the same problem.

Of course, if you have The

Hammer, your computer may never be safe. So maybe you should lock it up when you aren't around before you are heading out to replace your damaged computer!

Section V: Web Browsing Wonders

Chapter 10: I Didn't Click Yes!

Anyone in computer support has at one time or another run into that annoying malware that masks itself as malware and spyware remover for your computer. This malicious software will often pop up when you go to an infected website and ask you to install it to "Protect" your computer. In fact, this software is itself malicious and often slows down your computer to the point that is unusable and, in some cases; it can actually steal your personal data and history as well. These pieces of malware were all the rage for a few years and some even became smart enough to install automatically whether you answered yes or no to the question.

    Before they started doing that, however, you actually did have to click yes to install them. These pieces of malware were particularly troublesome to stop for a while because there wasn't any virus software out there that would stop them. They bypassed it all. Eventually anti-virus and anti-malware software caught up but for quite some time they were quite the pain. Many of my users were caught off guard by this type of software resulting in a computer that was slow and unresponsive taking their productivity down to zero. Of course, many of them denied installing anything at all.

It had been one crazy day. You know the days I'm talking about. It was a day of running around from one office to the next helping people. It was like everyone had gotten together and decided to break their computers all at once just to see how fast I could get everybody back up and running.

One of the benefits to days like that is how fast the day passes. Before I knew it, it was four in the afternoon. Only one more hour and the day will be finished. I can head home and turn on the television to catch up on what happened in the

Olympics that day. At least that's what I thought. Then my phone rang.

"This is Matt", I answered.

"Hey this is Bill."

"Hey Bill. How's it going?"

"Pretty good. How 'bout you?"

"Not too bad. What can I do for you?"

"Well something has popped up on my screen and now my computer is really slow."

"What is on your screen?"

"I don't know, some spyware cleaner thing. I wasn't doing anything and it just popped up out of nowhere."

"Nothing, huh." I knew better.

"Nope nothing", Bill said.

"Okay I will be up in just a minute. Don't click anything else."

"I won't."

With that I hung the phone up and headed up the stairs. I hurried because I knew the day was coming to an end and I didn't want to work late that day. As I walked I just hoped that it wouldn't be anything too serious.

"Hey Bill."

"Hey. See check this out", Bill said. "This scanner just popped up out of nowhere and started running as scan. Now, my computer is so slow I can't do anything and I can't click it to make it go away."

"Oh, looks like you got hit with a bit of spyware", I said.

This particular brand of spyware was annoying but it wasn't anything that couldn't be easily cleaned. It did take a bit of time to clean but I was more concerned with how Bill actually got it. I killed the spyware and began the slow process of cleaning it.

"You will be down for a bit. This takes some time to clean."

"How long?"

"Well, it's after four now so I would say sometime around five."

"That's not going to work I have to get something done by then."

"Sorry, that's the best I can do."

I could tell Bill was a bit irritated but there was honestly nothing I could do. The junk had to be removed and a spyware and virus scan had to be run to make sure everything was clean before he could work again. We had a bit of time so I thought I would try to discover exactly what Bill was up to when the spyware popped up on his screen.

"So, now what exactly were you doing when the spyware popped up?" I asked.

"Like I said, nothing", Bill responded quickly.

"Nothing at all?"

"Nope."

"So you weren't even touching your computer and it popped up?"

"Well....", Bill said with his voice trailing off.

"Well.... what?", I asked quickly.

"Okay I was on the Internet."

"Oh I see-"

"No it's not what you think", he interrupted. "I wasn't on anything I that we aren't allowed to be on. It's not like I was looking at porn."

"Then what were you doing?"

"Just looking at a few sites."

"Work related?", I asked. After a moment of silence I continued, "You can tell me or I will just look up the history and find out. Your choice."

"Okay, okay. It wasn't work related. I took a break to check out some of the up to date Olympic results. I wanted to know how we were doing before I watched it tonight."

"What site did you go to exactly?"

"I don't know. I just did a search and the site that came up had some funny characters on it that looked, I don't know, maybe Chinese or something."

"Oh now I see what happened."

"So I went somewhere I wasn't supposed to go?", he asked earnestly.

"Well yes and no."

"Huh?"

"Let me explain. Technically you didn't go anywhere that was against company policy but the site you did choose to look at could have been hacked so it would disperse the spyware or was designed just for that purpose. It's also possible that the code was embedded in one of the ads and the site has no idea that it is going on. I'm guessing that you didn't even have to click anything and the code ran on your computer automatically as soon as your browser loaded the site."

"See, I told you I wasn't doing anything."

"Technically, you aren't supposed to be reading sports results while working. But I will give you a pass on that assuming I can finish this before five."

"I hope so I don't want to work late", Bill replied.

"Neither do I!"

It took quite awhile for the scans to complete but a few minutes after five I had finished getting rid of the pesky little piece of spyware.

"Done."

"Great now I can finish my work. Maybe I will wait and do it tomorrow."

"Just do me a favor."

"What's that?"

"Don't go to that site ever again", I said.

"Don't worry. I won't ever go there again. I don't want to go to any site again."

"Well you don't have to be afraid of every site. Just steer clear of that one."

"Will do. Thanks."

"No problem at all", I said as I

walked out of Bill's office.

"So much for leaving at five today", I thought to myself as I made my way back to my office.

I hurried and did my best to get out of there as quickly as possible but there were still tasks that I had to complete before I could leave. These tasks would have normally been done during my last hour at the office but because somebody wanted to sneak a peak at the Olympic results I was stuck working for another hour. But, such is the life of an I.T. guy.

While anti-malware and anti-virus software has long since caught up with many of these types of spyware, there are still several out there that can catch an uninformed user off guard. Many times you don't even have to click yes on anything to cause the damage. By simply going to the site the code will execute and in some cases there isn't much you can do. If you run into this situation it is best to click on nothing and immediately close your browser and kill the applications. If you aren't sure what to do, don't touch anything and immediately call for help.

Above all, if this does happen to you, don't lie to the one you called for help. Be honest and tell them exactly what happened so they know the most likely cause. I realize that sometimes you may have gone somewhere you shouldn't have but these types of infections can happen even on legitimate sites and are out of your control. Just be honest and let your I.T. guy know how the events unfolded exactly so they can better troubleshoot your problem and get you fixed up much more quickly.

Chapter 11: Toolbar Blues

For quite awhile, it seems almost every developer out there got into the toolbar market releasing their own toolbar designed to work with your Internet browser. These toolbars all claimed to "enhance" your browsing experience but, in my opinion, all they did was slow everything down.

Add to that the fact that spammers and spyware makers got into the toolbar game and it didn't take long for toolbars to gain a bad reputation. This was often due to the fact that the installation of the toolbars would reset different aspects of your browser including your default homepage and even your search preferences. Some toolbars blocked your access to competitors altogether or just rerouted you to the spammer or spyware sites.

Now, while I long held the opinion that most of the toolbars were just junk and a waste of space on your computer there were many out there that loved them. I think some people even thought they had to have them in order to search the Internet. Some people loved them so much that they had to have every toolbar they could find.

In the company I was working for at the time there was a strict policy against installing anything on your computer that was not authorized by the I.T. department. We enforced this largely by not allowing any user to have admin rights to the computers. But, many toolbar makers found ways to exploit Windows so their toolbars would install regardless of the security settings on the machines. Whether you had the admin password or not, many of the toolbars would install anyway.

    I was walking through the halls of my company one afternoon heading back to my office after replacing a faulty hard drive on another computer when I received a page. I should clarify. The office in which I worked came equipped with a paging system in the building. There were speakers strategically placed all over the building so someone could track you down if they really needed you.

The very nature of my job meant that people heard my name over the paging system quite often as I didn't spend too much time at my desk. Over the years I learned to loathe the paging system mainly because of its abuse. Instead of people paging me when they really needed me, they would page me over every little thing.

For example, a computer that won't turn on is most definitely a page able reason even if many times it turns out they aren't even plugged in to the wall. But, paging me because they can't remember where the icon is for the Internet browser is not a good page able reason. Take two seconds to look and you will be amazed how easy it is to find.

Some people even stopped calling me altogether and only used the paging system to track me down. This was fine as long as I wasn't in my office, but if I was it was a problem. You see my office was located in the one area of the building that did not have good coverage by the paging system. If I was sitting at my desk I wouldn't even hear the page. This resulted in a lot of angry people thinking I was ignoring them.

As you can see, my hatred for the paging system was completely valid but I dealt with it the best that I could.

Anyway, I heard my name over the paging system with the request for me to call a specific extension number. Remembering phone numbers and extensions was always pretty easy for me to do, so I knew immediately who it was that was looking for me. It was Bill.

I walked to the closest phone I could find and dialed Bill to find out what was going on but there was no answer. Nothing annoyed me more. Why does someone page me and then not answer when I try to respond to the page. I tried again with no luck. So, I left the office I ducked into and continued my walk to my office.

I took about four steps when I heard Bill paging me again requesting me to call.

"Grrrrrr", I growled to myself. "If you need me answer your phone!", I thought to myself annoyed.

I ducked into the next office and called Bill again. This time, however, he decided to actually answer.

"Hey Matt."

"Hey Bill. What's up?", I asked.

"I have no Internet."

"Really?"

"I can't get to anything."

"Okay let me run check one thing and then I will head over to see you."

"Thanks."

I hung up the phone and hurried back to my office to check the Internet. I figured it was up otherwise I would really be getting paged from everybody. But I wanted to make sure just in case. I quickly opened up my browser and tried a couple of websites and they opened just fine. "It's not our Internet", I thought.

I hurried down the hall to Bill's office to see why he didn't have Internet.

"I can't go anywhere online and I need to do some research", he said as I walked in his door.

"That's weird. I stopped to test our Internet before coming over and it was working fine for me."

"Can you get to the fileserver?", I asked.

"Let me check."

There was a moment of silence as I waited for him to try the server.

"Yep I can get there just fine."

"Okay so you are still connected to the network. Open your browser for me."

"Here you go."

"See, you can't go anywhere."

I looked and was shocked by what I saw on the screen. Instead of a toolbar at the top and a nice open white space where the websites would normally load all I saw was row after row after row of toolbars. At the bottom there was a small line of what would have been the website but definitely not enough for you to be able to see and use.

"Why in the world do you have so many toolbars?", I asked.

"Toolbars?"

"Yes."

"I don't know what you mean. I've always had these."

"There is no way you always had these. I do not install these", I said.

"Well I have."

"If you did you would never have been able to look at websites. They don't leave enough room on your screen so you can."

"I don't know", he said.

"Well, I have to get rid of all these."

"But I need them to be able to go online."

"No you don't. You just think you do. Watch."

I could tell he was annoyed but I had to do something. So, one by one I went through each junk toolbar he had installed on his computer and removed them. Some were easier than others. For a few I even had to login as the administrator to remove them. It's funny, to install them you don't have to be an admin but to get rid of them you do.

A couple of the toolbars wouldn't even uninstall. I had to manually remove them and their registry entries just to make sure they were gone for good. After several minutes and listening to Bill impatiently ask, "How much longer?", every few minutes I was finally done. I gave the computer a quick reboot.

"Now everything should work fine."

"But how will I use the Internet without the toolbars?", he asked plainly.

"You don't need the toolbars to use the Internet. Some toolbars just give you extra functions and others are just plain junk. But you don't need any of them to actually work."

"If you say so."

"Trust me. Here, have a seat", I said.

The computer was now rebooted and waiting patiently at the log in screen for him to enter his username and password. He did and the computer came to life as expected.

"Now, open up your browser."

"Okay", he said as he double clicked on his desktop shortcut.

The browser opened and the

default homepage loaded very quickly just as I knew it would.

"Wow. That loaded fast. But I can't type in what I want without the toolbar."

"Yes you can. See the one main toolbar at the top. You can search in that box or you can go to the search page and type in whatever you want."

"Oh I see!", he said as a flash of understanding passed across his face. "This is much better. I can see so much more of the screen, too!"

"I told you that you could trust me", I said confidently.

"You were right. Thanks."

"Just don't install anymore of those toolbars again. You don't need them and we prohibit their installation."

"Okay I won't. Sorry, I thought I needed them."

"No problem. Trust me if you leave them all off your Internet will be much better."

"I can already tell a difference. Thanks!", Bill said.

"You're welcome. See you later."

"Take it easy", Bill replied.

With that, I headed back down to my office still shocked at how many different toolbars he had installed. Honestly, I lost count of how many it was total but there were at least ten different toolbars and not one of them was really necessary.

There are some toolbars out there that can be quite useful in certain circumstances. But, many of them are just junk designed to slow down your Internet and force you to use certain sites. With most modern day browsers, most of the functions of the good toolbars are already included and you just don't need them much at all anymore. But, some people still believe they are necessary and there are many toolbars still floating around out there that are designed to force you to use certain sites and some even slow down your computer and are simply considered spyware.

If I were you, I would avoid third-party toolbars altogether even if they come from a reputable company. These days there just isn't a need for them as modern browsers come with all the extra features they used to offer. For the most part, all you will find is junk software that slows down your Internet browser or forces you to use certain websites without your choice.

But, if you do decide that you must use third-party toolbars please don't install ten or more of them. You want to be able to see the websites you are looking at, after all.

Section VI: Sex, Lies and MPEGS

Warning

The following stories feature material that would be considered more adult in nature. The subject matter is not necessarily suitable for children. Like the other stories, all of the following stories are completely true. Names have been changed to protect the innocent and the guilty.

Chapter 12: Bathtub Backup

I was sitting in my office one afternoon repairing a computer with a broken hard drive when Claire knocked on my door.

"Hey", she said cheerfully.

"Hey, how's it going?", I asked.

"Pretty good. I was wondering if you had time to help me."

"Sure. What's up?"

"Well...It's not really work related."

"Okay. What is it?", I asked.

"See, I just got this new computer. I love it! It is so fast. My old computer is about to die so I'm so happy to have this new one."

"That's great. It's always fun to get a new computer. Of course, I'm a computer guy so I'm a bit bias."

"It really is, isn't it? Anyway, I need help moving all my files from the old computer to the new one. The truth is, I don't even know where most of the files are on the computer. Things are everywhere. So I need help so I don't lose any of my files. Especially my pictures and music."

"I can help you with that", I said. "I'm a bit busy at the moment so it might take me until tomorrow to get it done."

"Well, I don't have everything here but I will bring it in the morning. That okay?", she asked.

"Sure. Just come see me in the morning. Assuming things don't blow up here I'm sure I can get it done for you."

"Great! Thanks!"

She turned and headed out of my office. Now, quite often I get asked by people in the office to fix their personal computers. Many people seem to think that because you work for the company they work for that you are supposed to fix their personal computers as well. That, of course, isn't the case. But, most of the time I do it anyway just to be nice.

The next morning came as it always does and I had just sat down in my office when Claire came to my door holding a big, bulky desktop computer that looked like it was made in the '90's. You know the kind that I am talking about – the oversized, beige desktop that has yellowed over time. She was struggling a bit because of the weight and size of this behemoth.

"This is it", she said as she almost fell over setting the computer down at my door.

"Wow. Exactly how old is this thing?", I asked.

"Um, I'm not sure. Let's see...about...eight years old. I think."

"Well, you have gotten your money's worth out of this one."

"Yeah but now it is so slow. Oh my god. It takes forever just to turn on."

"Where is your new computer?"

"Oh. It's still in the car. Be right back."

"Okay."

As she headed back to her car I got up and picked up oversized computer and moved it to my workstation. It was solid, that's for sure. I don't know exactly how much it weighed but needless to say it was one of the heavier computers I have come across. I connected it to a monitor, keyboard and mouse and plugged it in. Just as I turned it on, Claire returned with her new computer under her arm.

"Here it is", she said.

"Oh I see you decided to go with

a laptop instead of another desktop."

"Yeah I wanted something I could take with me."

"You will enjoy it much more."

"I think so too. I see you turned the old one on already. See how long it is taking just to turn on."

I turned to look at the computer and, sure enough, it was still in the process of booting up. "This should be fun", I thought to myself because as slow as it was moving meant that it was going to take a bit of time to copy off her files.

"I see. It might take awhile for everything to copy given how slow it is. But, I will keep you posted on how things are going today."

"Thanks a lot."

"If I have any questions about any files I will let you know."

"You might have to look around there are picture files everywhere and I need to be sure I save them all."

"No problem. I will look around and track down all the pictures and music I can find. Do you have a lot of documents that you need as well?"

"Some. But I think they are all together."

"Well, I will check just to be safe", I said.

"Thanks. Just let me know", Claire said as she turned and headed out of my office.

I went over to my shelves and grabbed a spare external USB hard drive to use to backup her data and sat back down in my chair. The computer was still loading although I could now at least see a blank desktop picture. I went ahead and plugged in the external hard drive so everything was ready to go and turned to take care of some actual work while I waited for the relic to completely boot up.

After a few minutes the computer finally finished loading and I could see what I had to work with. She wasn't kidding. There were files all over her desktop. These files were pictures and regular documents. In addition, there were a ton of pictures and music where you would expect to see them. "No problem", I thought. This shouldn't take too long.

Quickly, I organized the random files I found into types and put them into folders to be copied. I then combined them with all the files that were actually stored where they were supposed to be stored. The computer was starting to look better already and everything was where it should be. The process took longer than I expected because she had thumbnail view turned on so the images were loading in a larger size. This increased the time it took to organize everything but I didn't bother to change it because it was only a few folders. It was only a few gigabytes worth of data including the pictures and the music so I knew the transfer wouldn't take too long even on an old computer like I was dealing with.

"Okay, now to look through everything to see if there is anything I missed", I thought.

I opened the C drive on her computer to see if anything had been saved there instead of the desktop. There were several folders that had very random names containing a mix of letters and numbers. I opened one of the folders and found hundreds of pictures stored in these folders.

Now it wasn't the fact that there were hundreds of pictures. It was what they were! Remember me saying that thumbnail view was on? These pictures were of Claire and they weren't pictures you would find on your favorite social media site. These were shots of Claire nude in a bathtub. I was shocked. Quickly I closed the window with the picture thumbnails on it. After all, I was sitting in my office at work and what would someone say if they walked in and saw that. I glanced around one last time to make sure no one was around.

    I have seen a lot of crazy things on people's computers throughout the years. But this was a first for me. I couldn't believe it. I just saw way more of Claire than I had ever planned to see. I sat there for a minute stunned. "Okay, what do I do?", I asked myself. "Do I tell her about them? Do I say anything? No. I will just copy the folders in with the other pictures and not say a word." With that thought, I moved all the pictures into a folder all their own and combined them with the rest of her pictures.

"Do I keep checking for my files? No I think I have found everything", I said to myself.

I then copied all of Claire's files that I had collected from all over her computer to the external hard drive that I had connected to the computer earlier. This was going to take a little bit of time so I turned to try to focus on a little work. I was still shocked at what I came across, though so I couldn't concentrate at all. Let's face it, you never expect to see pictures like that of your coworker. I turned to check the status of the copy and it was moving slowly as I expected. "Good", I thought. "This means that it will be awhile before I need to call her."

Finally my phone rang and I had to focus on work because people needed help. I left the old computer to copy the files as I left my office to take care of a problem Bill was having with his computer. I had never been so happy to get a phone call. I needed the distraction.

When I returned to my office the copy had finished. I don't know exactly how long it took to complete all I knew was it was done. I quickly shut down the old computer and disconnected the hard drive.

Claire's new computer was a pretty sweet looking laptop and it was every bit as fast as she boasted booting up in a matter of seconds instead of over five minutes like the old computer. I connected the hard drive to her new computer and carefully moved each type of file to its proper location including the private pictures I accidentally stumbled upon while backing up her old computer. It went much faster with the new computer and after several minutes every file was in its proper place.

    I picked up the phone and sat back in my chair for a moment before giving Claire a call. "I have to be casual and act like I haven't seen anything that I wasn't supposed to see."

    I dialed her extension and waited for her to answer.

    "This is Claire."

    "Hey Claire. This is Matt."

"Hey! How's my computer?

"It's good. I'm all done."

"That's great. I owe you a lunch."

"Thanks", I said with a chuckle. "I went ahead and organized the files too so you can find everything. All your music is in the music folder, your pictures are in the pictures folder, and so on."

"Oh thank you that will make it much easier."

"I think I got everything. But you will need to look through your files to be certain."

"Sounds good. I will come down later and pick everything up."

"Okay."

With that she hung up the

phone. "I played it cool. I saw nothing", I thought casually to myself.

The rest of the day passed without a hitch and right before the end of the day Claire came down to my office.

"Hey!", she said cheerfully. "Thanks so much for doing this for me. I really appreciate it."

"No problem. It didn't take long at all."

"Can you show me where all the files are?"

"Sure", I said hoping she wouldn't ask me about the private folders I made.

I clicked around her computer quickly showing her where each file type was stored. "And this is your picture folder. All your pictures are here." Quickly I closed the window with the pictures and showed her the files that were on her desktop. "I moved all the files that were on the desktop of your old computer into this folder here. You can save what you want and move things around from here."

"Oh that's perfect thank you."

"You're welcome. Any questions?"

"No I don't think so. I really do owe you lunch. What about next week?"

"Um, sure. Sounds good to me."

"Great."

"Would you like help getting

this stuff to your car?"

"Oh you don't have to do that."

"It's no problem", I said.

"Great. I'm just up front."

With that we gathered up her old and new computer and headed out the front door of the office to load her car. I slid her old computer in her backseat and closed the door.

"By the way, what do you plan on doing with your old computer?"

"I'm not sure. I might throw it away or recycle it."

"Well, if you do, bring it back here so we can destroy the hard drive properly."

"Why?"

"It still has your files on it and

we don't want strangers to have access to them."

"That's true", she said thoughtfully. "I will let you know what I decide and then maybe I can bring it back?"

"Sure."

"Great. Remember, lunch next week."

"Sounds good to me."

She hopped into her car and headed home. I went back into the building to finish up a couple of things before heading home myself. She never knew I accidentally came across those pictures. I'm sure she found them in all her pictures, though. If she thought I had seen them she never said anything about it. Of course, that's not something that is easily brought up.

"Hey how ya doing. Like my bathtub pictures?" See. It just doesn't work.

Computer guys see everything that is on your computer when you have them work on them. If you don't want them to even accidentally see something that you might find embarrassing, then it is best to get rid of it before you send your computer in for repair. The next time you turn your computer over to someone for help, remember this and get rid of anything that might be embarrassing before you drop it off. Computer guys won't necessarily go looking for the stuff, but it is very possible that they could stumble across it just like I did while they are trying to be helpful which can lead to an awkward moment for both of you.

Chapter 13: Husband's Secret

The cold morning was slowly morphing into a warm afternoon as I went about my normal day of running around the office helping people who broke their computer. As I walked back to my office I heard my name being called from down the hall. I paused for a moment to see Claire hurrying down the hall to catch up with me.

"It's okay you don't have to stop I will walk with you", she said.

"Okay", I said as I continued to walk.

"I was hoping I could talk you into doing me a favor?"

"That depends."

"On what?"

"What kind of mood I'm in", I said with a smile.

She smiled back. "I need you to look at my computer. Not the one here it's fine. My home computer."

"I see."

"What's going on with it?", I asked as we reached my office.

"It is just running really slow and I think the hard drive is full. We can't save anything on it."

"Do you have it here?"

"Why yes I do", she said with a grin.

"It's in my office. I will run grab it."

"Sounds good."

I took a quick glance at my emails to make sure nothing more pressing was happening while she was away. After a few minutes she returned with her desktop from her house. It was dusty and definitely had a bit of age on it.

"Look, I know this thing is old", Claire said. "But I'm not ready to buy a new one just yet."

"That's fine. So it is just running slow?"

"Slower than normal, yes. And we can't save anything to the computer."

"Well, leave it with me and I will take a look. I will run a few scans on it as well so it probably won't be finished today."

"No problem. I will check with you tomorrow", she said as she turned to head out my office door.

"Sounds good. Oh wait. Do you want me to delete any junk I find on here?"

"Yes. All our important files are in the My Documents folder everything else isn't important."

"Got it."

With that, she walked out of my office leaving me with her computer. I had a quiet moment so I hooked it up and turned it on. It booted up slowly but nothing to crazy. Once the desktop loaded I finally could see what she meant. It took forever to do anything. I managed to open the hard drive and that's when I saw that there was only 100 megabytes worth of free space.

    For those of you that don't know, while you may have 1000 gigabytes worth of space on your computer, that doesn't mean you can take up every last byte of memory. Computers use the hard drive to store temporary files that help speed up the machine and without these your computer will slow down to a crawl.

    I still wanted to run a scan of the computer to make sure it was virus and malware free, but it would take hours with the computer in this shape. I knew I was going to have to free up some hard drive space first before I could do anything else. First, I cleared the desktop of anything that was large. There were a few movies and some pictures. After clearing the desktop I managed to free up about 500 megabytes. I checked the size of their My Documents and found it wasn't very big at all. Sure, there were some pictures and a few home movies but it wasn't large at all yet they had a three hundred and twenty gigabyte hard drive.

    I got a little crazy from there and scoured the folders deleting every temporary file I could find. No matter what I did I just couldn't free up enough space on the hard drive to make any real difference. There weren't very many applications installed on the computer. Just the usual web browser and office suite so there was nothing I could remove there. So what exactly was taking up all the space?

It was then that I stumbled across it. I noticed under her husband's account a folder named Untitled. In that folder was another folder called Untitled and then another folder. "Strange", I thought to myself. It seemed like the Untitled folders would never end. Then, all of a sudden I found where all their hard drive space went. After about twenty or so folders I hit the mother load of files. There were literally thousands of pictures and movies in there. I took a quick glance at one of them and let me tell you these weren't pictures of their kids. Think of them more as inspiration for baby making. Have you guessed it now? Porn! There was so much porn hidden in there that all of their hard drive space had been taken. This guy had a serious addiction.

"Great", I thought. "Now what am I going to do." I couldn't tell her that her husband has a secret porn fetish. No way am I going to get in between their marriage. But this computer needs some space so it can actually be used. I decided to sort the porn by file size and get rid of the biggest files to free up space. Yes I know I was deleting this guy's collection but really this was insane. I must have cleared half of the collection and with that came 100 gigabytes of precious hard drive space freed up.

"Now we are getting somewhere", I thought. "Time to scan the computer. With this much porn this computer is bound to have a virus or two."

    I proceeded to run a virus and malware scan on the computer. This took quite a bit of time but I just let it run and went about my normal day. The afternoon began to wind down just as the scans had completed. Sure enough, there were several viruses and malware on the computer. I cleaned them and rebooted computer. It booted much faster now and there was plenty of space to work. As I was performing a few last minute checks on the computer my phone rang.

    "Hey. It's Claire. How's my computer?"

    "It's running much better now. I cleared off a lot of useless files especially in your husband's account."

"What kind of stuff?"

"Oh, just the normal junk that accumulates over time. Nothing to worry about."

"Great. Did it have a virus?"

"Yes it did. But that is cleared up now, too. I just have one quick thing to do. I will be done by the time you get here if you want to come over and grab it."

"Perfect. I will be right there."

While I waited for her to show up at my door I made one little change on the computer. Just as I was closing out the computer Claire knocked on my door.

"Hey. I was just about to shut it down."

"Thanks a lot for doing this",

she said.

"No problem at all", I said as I unhooked her computer. "Here you go."

She picked up the computer and began walking to the door. "I owe you big time."

"It's no problem at all. I think you will find it is running much better now."

"Thanks. See you later", she said as she turned to head back to her desk.

"You're welcome."

Success. I was able to clean the computer and I didn't have to tell her what her husband was up to. Looking back on it maybe I should have told her. But I really didn't want to be a part of that discussion at all and I didn't want to embarrass her by telling her either. I will tell you this. Her husband discovered pretty quickly that I knew what he was up to, though. Not only was he missing some of his stash, but remember that last change I told Claire about? I changed the folder name of that last folder from "Untitled" to "Look What I Found".

    Claire never asked me to work on another computer of hers again but her husband was always really nice to me whenever I saw him with Claire outside the office. It's funny how someone will react when you find their stash of porn.

    I'm not here to judge. What you

look at online is your business. But, if you do like to keep a collection of downloads from the Internet, just make sure they don't eat up every last byte of your hard drive. That's really not necessary especially these days when you can just stream whatever you want online. If you do run out of space, check your downloads before taking it somewhere to be worked on. You might be able to solve your own problem without needing a computer guy to go through your computer with a fine-toothed comb.

Chapter 14: Executive V"P"

I came rushing into the office one morning late because traffic had been particularly bad that day. I was a fresh out of college and it was only my second week on the job so I was worried that I might be in trouble for being late. When I finally reached my desk I realized that I wasn't the only one that got stuck in the traffic so I began to breathe a little easier. My boss wasn't even there yet.

I sat down at my desk and turned my computer on ready to start the day. I looked up and saw Bill, the Executive Vice President walking toward me. This guy rarely ever left his office but we all knew whom he was. He was the number two man in the company and he had a bit of a reputation. He was well known for forcing people out of the company if he didn't like you. Well, let's just say that was the rumor. I never saw any actual proof of someone being forced out because he/she was on Bill's bad side while I was there. But I had been there only two weeks and all I had heard at the time were the rumors that floated around the office gossip channels.

    He seemed to be looking for one of the other techs in the office but because of the traffic I was the only one that was there. After exhausting his search around the department he finally walked up to my desk.

    "You're Matt, the new guy, right?", he asked quickly.

"Yes sir. Nice to meet you", I replied.

"Yes, you too. I am having trouble with my computer. I don't know exactly what is going on with it but the damn thing just isn't cooperating at all. I was looking for Bill to help me but he doesn't seem to be here yet."

"No I think he is stuck in that traffic with everyone else it seems like."

"Well you and I made it here alright."

"Just barely, sir."

He smiled. "True I just walked in myself."

"So your computer is acting up?", I asked.

"Yes it is."

"Is it slow or are programs not opening?"

"It's very slow. I can't get my email open either."

"Okay just let me find someone to let them know where I will be and I will head right up."

"Great."

I looked around the department to try to find somebody to inform before I headed up to Bill's office but no one was around. They were all either off working on something else or still stuck in the traffic nightmare that was taking place on the streets. Finally I gave up and sent my boss a quick email so no one would be searching for me. I then headed up to the Executive Vice President's office.

I arrived at the door and buzzed to be let in. You see, at the first company I worked for the Executive Offices were behind closed, locked doors away from the "normal" employees. I never understood why it was like this. It seemed like they were afraid of an employee going postal or something like that. After a few seconds one of the office assistants buzzed me in and I walked in the door.

"Hey Matt! Good morning", Claire said cheerfully.

"Hi. I'm here to see Bill. He is having computer issues."

"Oh yes. You can head right in."

"Thanks."

His door was open so I walked up and knocked on the frame. "Hey Bill."

"Hey thanks for coming to take a look."

"No problem at all. Mind if I have a seat at your computer?"

"Sure thing. It's really slow and I can't open anything at all."

"Okay. What were you doing when it started?", I asked.

"Oh look at the time. I have to head to a meeting. Think you can take it from here?"

"No problem. I will figure it out. How long is your meeting?"

"It will be most of the morning so you have plenty of time", Bill said.

"Great. I should be ready by the time you come back unless I find something major wrong with it."

"Thanks", Bill replied as he walked quickly out the door.

I shook my head and turned around to look at his computer. He had one of the few laptops in the building. At that time, laptops were reserved for only those who travelled extensively and for the top brass of the company. Everybody else had to live with a normal desktop. I moved the mouse of his computer and I could hear the hard drive spin as I moved the cursor. I tried to open a couple of pieces of software but nothing really happened. The hard drive was spinning like mad but nothing was loading. Finally, after a few minutes the first program I attempted to open loaded onto the screen.

"Well, at least it is sort of working", I said under my breath.

I opened the C drive of the computer and took a look. Like so many others, the hard drive was full. "Great", I thought to myself. "How am I supposed to know what is okay to delete and what isn't. And why isn't he saving his files to the server?"

I poked around a little more and couldn't find anything that was of any value. He had no documents, no pictures, nothing. Even he didn't have the admin rights to install a bunch of software without talking to me first so I knew he hadn't been loading his own applications. What could be taking up so much space?

I began searching out the various temporary file locations on his computer. There were a few files but nothing too crazy. Finally I reached the temporary Internet files. Whoa! This thing was full! There were so many files there were too many to count. There were cookies and picture files that went on for what seemed like forever when I scrolled through them. Of course, while the amount of files was surprising, it was the type of files that were the most startling.

It seems that Bill, Mr. Executive Vice President was more like Bill, Mr. Executive Vice Perv. There were hundreds of thousands of cookies and picture files for virtually every type of porn you can think of. But, it seems he was particularly fond of a two different types based on the cookies and the frequency of the addresses that appeared in them. They appeared so often it looked to me like he had a subscription to these particular sites. What were his favorite sites? Are you sure you want to know? Okay, you talked me into it. They were Little Asian Asses and Pee Fetish!

Once I ran into the second one I was sick to my stomach. Now, I don't care what you look at in the privacy of your own home. But to be looking at sites like these on your work computer is gross and just plain wrong.

"Oh my god", I said as I looked

through all the smut on his work computer. "Okay what do I do?", I asked myself. I was still new at this company and I was dealing with the number two guy in charge of things. Do I say anything to anyone? Should I delete this stuff? Typical questions you ask when you are brand new and very young.

After a few moments I decided that because of company policy I would have to delete the files. I grabbed one of the nastier cookie files and placed it on the desktop and then deleted everything else that was in the folder. Next I ran a scan of the computer to verify that there were no viruses and I restarted the computer. Luckily, there were no viruses on the machine and just freeing up the hard drive space took care of the problem. I left that one little file on his desktop, though.

I walked out of the office and told the assistant Claire that everything was working fine on his computer now. "Just let Bill know I fixed it", I said. "Tell him I left an important file for him on his desktop and to call me if he has any problems."

A few hours passed and I was back at my desk taking care of my normal work when Bill payed me a little visit.

"Claire told me you fixed it. I appreciate it. I was able to open my email no problem", Bill said.

"Great. Just let me know if you have anymore issues."

243

"Thanks I will. Oh and if you are ever walking by the offices stop in. You can grab a drink from our private fridge. We have all types of soda, tea and our own coffee if you like."

"That would be great. Thanks a lot", I said.

I never told anybody about what I found on Bill's computer. It worked out for everybody, though. Bill got his computer fixed and didn't get in trouble for violating company policy and I got access to the Executive kitchen with all the goodies and drinks that I wanted. Did I take advantage of that? Of course I did. What good, self respecting I.T. guy wouldn't take advantage of free food and drinks whenever they got the chance?

Virtually every company in the world has some policy banning the use of pornographic websites using company computers. But, you might be surprised exactly how many people are so addicted to pornography that they even have to look at it while they are at work. I have actually found porn on people's computers who sit in an open area. How they managed to look at it without anyone seeing is beyond me.

Personally, I don't care if you like to look at it or not. But, if you do, just keep it on your home computer. Don't come to work and start looking at porn. Many of the pornographic sites are loaded with viruses and malware that can really mess up your computer. Of course, if you are caught looking at porn at the office, your computer's health might be the least of your worries as it could be grounds for dismissal. Bill was lucky, he was pretty high up the food chain at the company I worked for and I was young and relatively new to the corporate world. But, you might not be so lucky. So you better think twice before opening pornographic websites at your company, you could be in for more problems than you ever bargained for.

Conclusion

I hope you enjoyed these stories from my time in tech support. Over the last fifteen years I have run into some truly funny and ridiculous situations. I hope these stories made you laugh or at least smile and I hope they taught you a thing or two about your computer and how to deal with your company's tech guy or girl in the process.

Almost everyone has asked a silly question when it comes to computers at least one time in their life. Even tech guys run into silly situations and forget to check the plugs every now and then. These stories, while embarrassing, have happened to everybody and are a great way to learn a little more about computers and get an insight into how people react in certain situations.

These stories are only a mere sample of some of the crazy things that have happened to me over the last fifteen years in tech support. I hope this book to be the beginning of a series of books covering many of the funniest and craziest moments I have ever dealt with during my time in the corporate world. I hope each and every one of you enjoyed these stories and learned a little something in the process.

Thank you so much for taking the time to read these stories and I hope you all enjoyed them and learned a little something along the way. Until the release of the next book, I wish you all the best and remember to always check the plugs and reboot before calling your tech guy. And if you do have to call him/her, be sure to cooperate and tell the truth. It's the easiest way to get back up and running quickly without the pains and headaches that were experienced by both the users and me I dealt with in these stories. If you are exceptionally wise, cultivate a relationship with your tech guy in the office. It will make your life that much easier down the road when you do run into problems.

Printed in Great Britain
by Amazon.co.uk, Ltd.,
Marston Gate.